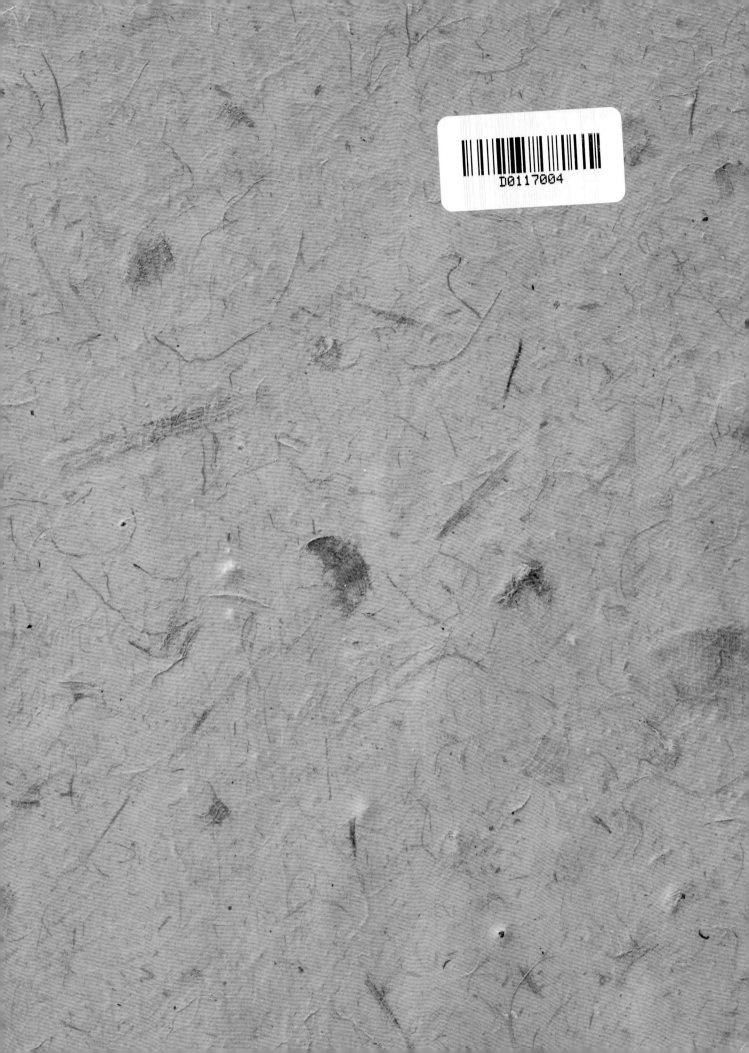

One Taste

Vegetarian Home Cooking from Around the World

By Sharon Louise Crayton

FOREWORD BY DZONGSAR JAMYANG KHYENTSE

PHOTOGRAPHS BY ERIC SWANSON

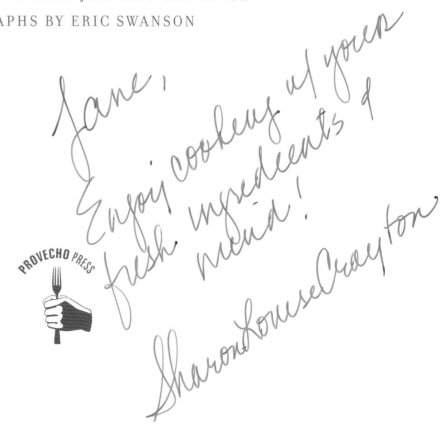

Jane,

Enjoy cooking up your fresh ingredients & mind!

Sharon Louise Crayton

PROVECHO PRESS

Designed by Maria Hwang Levy
Photography © Eric Swanson
All recipes © Sharon Louise Crayton
Published by Provecho Press, Santa Fe, New Mexico
Printed in China
First Edition 2008

ISBN 0-9719364-4-7

www.provechopress.com

"Once you recognize the true nature of mind,
this whole fiction of relative appearances and
your attachment to them will simply cave in.
Good and bad, pure and impure
lose their compelling flavors and
melt into one taste."

—H. H. DILGO KHYENTSE RINPOCHE

CONTENTS

Photo: Sandra Scales

Foreword

~~~~~~~~~~~~~~~~~~~~

The precious human body is a vessel that takes us to the shores of enlightenment. As we cross this ocean of existence, nurturing and maintaining our physical condition becomes an important part of the enlightenment process.

Taming the mind, as the Lord Buddha taught, is of supreme virtue. Feeding the body—which our mind relies on for support—is therefore an undeniable part of our practice.

From the perspective of Tantra, the body is the domain of the deities, the very mandala itself. So the act of eating, for a Tantric practitioner, becomes an act of *puja*, an offering to the body deities and a restoring of the sacred mandala within.

I hope the 108 recipes gathered here will help us to tame our minds, make offerings to the body mandala, and nurture the health of this body-vessel as we pursue the path of enlightenment. May this book create auspicious causes and conditions to taste and understand the myriad flavors in each moment of this life.

DZONGSAR JAMYANG KHYENTSE

La Sonnerie

Dordogne, France

Introduction

~~~~~~~~~~~~~

Many of us enjoy cooking and sharing our creations with family and friends. However, cooking brings with it a certain amount of pressure and expectation, especially with the busy lives most of us lead. Three times a day one must put on the table food that is nutritious, delicious, and satisfying. Over and over even the best cooks ask themselves the same questions and have the same thoughts: What shall I make tonight? I want everyone to love it. I want it to be delicious. Shall I try a new recipe or stick with a tired but tried-and-true fallback? Do I have all the ingredients? How can I get this on the table quickly? Even the greatest chefs admit that cooking is at times a chore.

For many years now I have been cooking for friends and family. It is not always an easy day-to-day job, especially when I feel many more important things are pressing, and to be honest I can't say I have always enjoyed it. I didn't know anything about preparing food until I was in my early twenties. When I realized the chore wasn't going away, I determined to learn how to do it well. In the process, I took in so many ideas about what constitutes the exotic and the nutritious that I grew confused and fearful. Was this onion organic? Could cheese be a part of a healthful diet? Am I going to gain or lose weight by eating these foods? Why don't the dishes I prepare look like the ones featured in magazines? The endless choices at the grocery store were daunting, as was our overflowing refrigerator, and I felt discouraged by the dirty dishes at the end of a less than satisfying meal.

In fact I was not really cooking at all. I was completely caught up in my expectations for perfect, specific results—a slave to my shoulds, coulds, and woulds. Over time I realized that maybe the problem was not the task of cooking itself but the attitude I had toward this universal and essential activity.

So I went back to basics—it didn't have to be complicated. My Buddhist meditation teacher, Dzongsar Khyentse Rinpoche, said, "Cook and eat as if you are going to die tomorrow. Let go of hope, fears, and obsessions. Simply appreciate what you have this moment." Reflecting on this allowed me to gradually peel away the layers of ideas and attitudes I had about food and cooking. I began to tame my mind, using the meditation method described in this book. I learned to enjoy whatever was happening. With new confidence, I returned to the kitchen, unencumbered by expectations and obsessions. Now I just cook, trying my best to stay in the present, to serve, and to let whatever happens happen.

I also learned from an old Breton chef named Josephine Araldo. After her family was killed in the First World War, she devoted her life to cooking for others. Her kitchen was small, unglamorous, and not particularly clean, but the food that came out of it was wonderful. She told me, "Do you know the mystery of good cooking? It is common sense." Josephine taught me to take everything out of the fridge in the morning, look at the ingredients with no preconceived ideas, and imagine what could be made. She believed it was better not to measure too precisely. She would dip her spoon into the salt and dump the crystals onto my open palm. "There, that is a tablespoonful—don't forget it!" Just taste the food as you cook, she would say, and adjust accordingly along the way. She made lots of mistakes, but they didn't bother her; she would simply revise her original plan and come up with something else. Cooking is trusting yourself.

In my years of travel, I have talked to many people in different cultures about their ideas of home cooking—not what they cook to impress company, but the no-fuss dishes that are most beloved. "What do you cook that your family loves best?" I ask. At first they are reluctant to answer, or their minds go blank. They cook these wonderful, satisfying dishes without much thought or effort. Then, after a moment of reflection, they are able to share. In this book I offer the recipes from their tables, their traditions, their cultures, and their families. They reflect an abundance of ideas and attitudes about how to prepare dishes and what tastes good.

This book captures the everyday cooking that satisfies again and again—the staples, the perfected favorites—and the meditation that is as much nourishment as the food itself. Along with each recipe, I have included a "Fresh Mind" meditation, which I hope will help you stay present and enjoy the process of cooking. My wish is that you will be inspired to experiment, so that when there is no recipe and it's just you, the cupboard, and the fridge, you can confidently rely on yourself to create a delicious meal. Have fun with the flavor wonders in the kitchen, and remember to appreciate what is on the table today.

Sharon L. Crayton

Kitchen Wisdom

Use the utensils of your mind to
Stir the pot of presentness
Mix the dough of mindfulness
Sharpen the knife of awareness
Wash the glass of perceptions and
Serve from the kitchen of loving kindness.

CHAPTER 1

Meditations

for One Taste

❁

Fresh Ingredients, Fresh Mind

What does it mean to cook with a fresh mind? The key to good cooking is not only to use fresh seasonal ingredients, but to approach them with a fresh mind and attitude. A fresh mind is natural, adaptable, relaxed, confident, and creative. With these qualities comes an appreciation of whatever is happening in the present moment, including our attitude toward the process of cooking. The expectations and obsessions that often accompany the task then fall away, and we are able to revel in the preparing and eating of wonderful dishes.

"Fresh Mind" meditation is a method of training our wandering minds by concentrating on an object. This object can be a mental state, such as patience, or the present moment's breath. The "Mind Refreshers" in this book aim to give our minds space to breathe, free of everything artificial and polluting, including the preconceptions and judgments we have absorbed from culture, society, teachers, and family.

We tend to see the world through a filter of habitual emotions and interpretations. First we have a feeling, then we have ideas about it, and then we act. We see an object of desire—cheesecake, for example—we are filled with longing for it, we determine we must have it, and then we devour it. Or, on the other hand, at the end of a long day when we are tired and have to cook for our family, we become irritated, we want to escape the obligation, and we order takeout instead, or we do cook but we resent it. We are always looking through a lens tainted by desire, jealousy, pride, anger, or delusions. Having no control over our minds, we are slaves to our thoughts and feelings. As Buddha said, "With our perceptions we make the world."

Even during meditation our minds are very busy and wandering, but they are much busier before and after meditation—we just do not realize it at first. Simply recognizing that our minds are busy and wandering is progress. Rejoice when you start to become aware of all the thoughts that crowd your mind. They were always there, but most of us are too busy creating bigger and bigger shopping lists to notice what is actually in the shop. With regular practice of Fresh Mind meditation, you will slowly begin to notice a calmer mind and an increasing ability to appreciate the infinite flavors of whatever is happening in the moment, even while facing all the distractions. Make it your aim to do lots of short Mind Refresher sessions throughout your day, and eventually the practice will become natural and habitual.

"In the beginning it is not easy; in the middle it is not very stable; in the end it becomes natural," as H. H. Dilgo Khyentse Rinpoche, meditation master of all the Tibetan Buddhist traditions, said. Meditation, like cooking, takes patience and practice.

a blue flower
a spoon
your breath or step
a morsel of chocolate
an herb on your counter
a red stoplight

Fresh Mind Meditation Recipe

The Fresh Mind or Shamatha meditation is a simple and practical method that works no matter what spiritual tradition you follow. You can employ this technique anywhere and at any time, without interfering with whatever it is you may be doing.

This meditation helps to loosen the grip that our emotions and the objects of our emotions have on us. By taming our minds, we can stay more relaxed and focused throughout the day's menu of events. We can keep a fresh mind with regard to whatever is happening, be it tasting our food, standing in the grocery line, or simply being with our bodies. Consider this practice a lovely thirty-second spa vacation. Don't cling to past experience. Don't anticipate the future. Remain appreciating the present.

METHOD
· Choose an object in your immediate surroundings.
· Sit or stand with your back straight.
· Relax and breathe normally.
· Watch the object.
· Concentrate on the object while your thoughts run here and there.
· Keep returning your mind to the object.
· There is nothing else to do.

COOKING TIME
Do lots of short sessions in a day, from thirty seconds to a few minutes. Once a week, allow yourself a fifteen- to thirty-minute session. Make this practice a habit; relax into the routine of these Mind Refreshers.

AFTER COOKING
Enjoy your freshened mind by appreciating whatever is happening in the moment.

SUGGESTIONS FOR SPECIFIC SITUATIONS
Walking, running, exercising: Use your step or breath.
At work: Use a tool of your craft.
At a coffee bar, dinner party, store, or nightclub: Use an object within your sight or your breath.

Patience

Keep it simple. Don't get excited when good things happen. Certain days are excellent; other days, no matter what you do, you can't concentrate. Do not get frustrated. Try again later.

You must taste the flavor of this Fresh Mind meditation at least once. Then, when doubt, boredom, and loneliness creep in, you will not lose motivation and enthusiasm to continue. You will resist the urge to throw the method away and search for another. Do longer sessions when you have time—half a day, a full day, three days, or more. Then, during your regular thirty-second sessions, you will know what you will get.

— Dzongsar Khyentse Rinpoche

Developing Habits

One develops any habit the same way one develops a drinking habit. How does one become an alcoholic? It is never by drinking six bottles of whiskey in one sitting. If one did that, one would get sick and never want to look at a drink again. No, it happens slowly, in small increments.

First your friend takes you to a bar and buys you your very first drink. You take a sip and don't really like it, but with encouragement and coaxing you try again. The second time is not quite as bad. Slowly you get used to it. You still don't really like it, but something about it begins to grow on you. Soon you feel the effects, and you like them. You find yourself drinking on an increasingly regular basis. It has become a habit.

Meditation is just like that. By doing lots of small sessions over time, it eventually becomes a habit. One day you will taste the taste of meditation, and it will come without effort.

— Dzongsar Khyentse Rinpoche

Mind Chatter

A friend was relaying her latest boyfriend drama and all the infinite possibilities of what would, could, or might happen.

"Namtok," I said, "is the Tibetan word for our thoughts or mind chatter."

"Lamp chops?!?"

"No, namtok!" I said.

"Umm," she said. "Then I'd better become a vegetarian!"

— International Girls Kitchen

The Art of Cappuccino Meditation

Too busy for a cappuccino? If not, you've found time for meditation.
Try doing this practice:

- Select a day and time for your regular weekly Cappuccino Meditation.
- Order your cappuccino or the beverage of your choice.
- Lift the cup to your lips and smell the aroma of the coffee.
- Marvel at the moment as the warm, seductive brew glides down your throat. You have just accomplished the unexpected. Because what if the ceiling had collapsed, or your breath had stopped? You would have missed your cappuccino moment. But you were there, if only for one moment.
- Continue to drink slowly. While you might normally have finished the whole thing in five gulps, now take ten or fifteen sips, giving yourself time.
- Watch the drink decrease and remember how a moment ago your cup was brimming to the top with milky foam.
- Observe that the cappuccino in your cup is going down and your stomach is filling up. The warm, seductive drink you once relished is now being digested in your stomach and will soon pass through you as a foul yellowish liquid. You will forget about the cappuccino and won't bother to think twice about what you once savored in your cup.
- Think how utterly ridiculous it is that you agonize, still, about the health virtues of brown sugar versus white sugar, skim versus whole milk, and just this is the point.
- Allow the sense of impermanence to arise in your mind. Knowing impermanence is the key to freedom. It lets us be less worried about our bodies growing older each day, our best china breaking, our good friend letting us down, being depressed, or being forever stuck with a habit or situation. It allows us to relax.

After six months of doing your weekly Cappuccino Meditation, getting your regular cappuccino with cinnamon, once a big deal, becomes a nonissue. When there is no cinnamon, you say matter-of-factly, "Ah, cappuccino without cinnamon, then," and that is that. Just this is a significant achievement. Simple though it sounds, the drinking of a cappuccino with awareness will create profound changes in your life.

—Dzongsar Khyentse Rinpoche

CHAPTER 2

Soups

for Infinite Flavors

Souper Douper Story

There is an old story of pilgrims lost in the wilderness, sheltering in a dark cave from a storm. When they were down to their last morsels of food, one of them had a great idea: if everyone put their scraps of food into one pot, they could make a hearty soup. As the cave filled with smoke from the fire, no one could see what each had to contribute or, cunningly, not contribute. While the soup was cooking, each pilgrim dreamed of how it would taste. Finally the soup was ready, and with great anticipation everyone was served. Each pilgrim took a deep slurp of the soup they had dreamed about. Everyone enjoyed their soup until one by one they woke up to the fact that the taste was . . . hot water!

Life is just like soup—it has so many different ingredients. Just as water alone is not soup, an onion alone is not soup, a single carrot is not soup, herbs are not soup; soup is the sum total of all its ingredients. So where is the soup? There is no inherent soupiness, except when you're in it!

— **YVONNE GOLD**, *English*

M any cultures serve soup as the evening meal because it is undemanding, comforting, and easy to digest. Created from leftovers and whatever is in season, soup isn't fancy. Vegetable soups made with water instead of stock develop the delicious taste of the vegetables rather than being overpowered by the taste of stock. A soup can take just fifteen minutes if the pieces are cut small. The texture and cooking time vary depending on whether you grate, dice, or coarsely chop the vegetables. Blending the soup at the end will also affect flavor and texture. Thicken soup by adding rice, polenta, thin noodles, shredded potato, oatmeal, roasted flour, cream, yogurt, couscous, or a roux (a little soft butter mixed with an equal amount of flour). Soup requires no big effort to make. You put the ingredients in the pot and they cook while you do the washing up.

1 cup (200 g) whole mung beans

6 cups (1½ L) water

2 teaspoons ground cumin

2 teaspoons ground allspice

2 teaspoons sea salt

2 medium tomatoes, diced (about 1 cup)

2 tablespoons fresh lemon juice

generous handful chopped fresh cilantro leaves (about ¼ cup)

1 teaspoon toasted sesame seed oil

Curried Mung Bean Soup

Middle Eastern

A Turkish woman, who was a yoga teacher, gave me this recipe. She would teach her class, then go into the kitchen and make this soup or something equally delicious with little effort. Her kitchen had a sense of simple design and warmth. The beans are cooked with the spices; at the end the soup is given a fresh lift with the addition of tomato, lemon, cilantro, and a hint of roasted sesame seed oil. Mung beans, small and green-skinned, are easy to digest and found at Asian grocers. In an Indian kitchen, the skinless, split mung beans are used for dal, called *moong dahl*. The allspice seasoning combines cloves, cinnamon, nutmeg, and ginger. The combination of allspice and cumin seed is known as "poor man's curry" seasoning.

METHOD

· Rinse mung beans in a colander under running water to remove dirt.
· Put mung beans, water, cumin, allspice, and salt in a large saucepan, over high heat, and bring to a boil.

Mind Refresher ✿ Stand straight, breathe normally, and concentrate on the moment's breath, in and out, 3 times. If you lose it, it doesn't matter; just breathe and concentrate.

· Stir mung beans, reduce heat to low, cover, and cook 1 hour or until beans are tender.
· Add more water if soup is too thick.
· Stir in tomatoes, lemon juice, cilantro, and sesame seed oil just before serving, to retain their fresh flavor. Season with more salt as needed.

Serves 4

Cream of Red Pepper Soup

North American, from California

This recipe comes from Café Sparrow, a restaurant I co-owned in the coastal town of Aptos, California. The spirit of the restaurant was full of fun. This recipe comes from my partner, who loved to wear her pink fuzzy slippers in the kitchen and even when greeting customers. The cream soup, always made with a seasonal vegetable, was a real crowd pleaser and a home favorite as well. In the fall, when red peppers are in season, this soup can't be beat. Rich, creamy, and rose-colored, with a hint of spice, it is served with a floating crouton, a dollop of sour cream, and a sprinkle of parsley.

METHOD

- Heat oil in a soup pot, over medium-high heat.
- Add onion, peppers, potatoes, and garlic; cook 5 minutes, stirring occasionally, to release flavors.
- Stir in parsley, cumin, cayenne, and salt; cook a few more minutes.
- Pour in water and bring to a boil.
- Reduce heat to low, cover, and cook 45 minutes, or until vegetables are tender.
- Transfer mixture to an electric blender or food processor. Blend with heavy cream and butter until smooth and thick. Pour soup back into pot.

Mind Refresher ✿ Stand straight, breathe normally, and taste the soup. Observe how it tastes and feels in the mouth. Focus on these sensations for 30 seconds.

- If too thick after blending, add a little more water. Cook, over medium heat, to blend flavors. Season to taste with salt.
- Spoon into soup bowls. Garnish each portion with a crouton, a dash of sour cream, and a sprinkle of parsley.

Serves 4

CROUTONS

Croutons go well in vegetable soups that do not have other grains in them. They can also be used in salads or as appetizers with spreads. Slice a French baguette or day-old bread into pieces about 1 inch (2.5 cm) in diameter. Place on a cookie sheet and bake at 400°F (200°C) for 8 to 10 minutes, or until light brown. An alternate method is to heat a little butter in a skillet over medium heat, add the bread cubes, and cook, stirring, until lightly browned. Store extras in the freezer.

2 tablespoons olive oil or vegetable oil

1 large onion, peeled and cut into 1-inch (2.5-cm) pieces (about 2 cups)

4 medium red bell peppers, seeded and cut into 1-inch (2.5-cm) pieces (about 4 cups)

5 medium Yukon gold or white potatoes (1½ pounds [750 g]), peeled and cut into 1-inch (2.5-cm) pieces (about 3 cups)

2–3 cloves garlic, peeled and finely chopped

handful fresh flat-leaf parsley, finely chopped (about ¼ cup)

1 teaspoon ground cumin

¼ teaspoon ground cayenne, or to taste

1 teaspoon sea salt

4 cups (1 L) water

½ cup (125 ml) heavy cream

2 tablespoons (60 g) butter

croutons

sour cream

fresh flat-leaf parsley, finely chopped

NOODLE DOUGH

NOODLE DOUGH
1½ cups (225 g) all-purpose flour
½ cup (125 ml) tepid water

SOUP
2 tablespoons olive oil or
    vegetable oil
1 medium onion, peeled and diced
    (about 1 cup)
1 small turnip, peeled and diced
    (about 1 cup)
½ head small green cabbage or
    cauliflower, finely chopped
    (about 2 cups)
4 ounces (125 g) fresh spinach
    leaves, well rinsed and roughly
    chopped (about 2 cups)
2 cloves garlic, peeled and finely
    chopped
1 teaspoon sea salt
10 cups (2½ L) water, divided:
    (6 cups [1½ L] and 4 cups
    [1 L])
2 tablespoons soy sauce or tamari

Tibetan Vegetable Noodle Soup

Tibetan, from the Amdo region

Thenthuk is the Tibetan name for the steaming bowls of hot noodle soup commonly eaten in the food tents in Bodgaya, India, the place of Buddha's enlightenment. Served at breakfast, lunch, and dinner, using any vegetables, *thenthuk* is also one of the most popular soups in Tibetan homes. The noodles are handmade, then cooked in broth for some time, giving the soup substance and the noodles a chewy consistency. If you don't want to bother making the noodles, substitute fresh wide egg noodles (about 5 ounces or 150 g), cut into pieces and added in the last ten minutes of cooking. Serve with a very hot chili sauce and soy sauce.

METHOD

NOODLE DOUGH
- Put a third of the flour in a medium bowl.
- Slowly add a third of the water, working mixture with your hand.
- Add more flour and water and work into dough.
- Add remaining flour and enough water to make a mass that holds together.
- On a well-floured board, knead the dough by hand in a fold and press motion to develop gluten, 2 minutes, or until not sticky and a finger hole stays indented.
- Cover with a towel; let rest 15 minutes.

Mind Refresher ❂ Before cutting the vegetables, stand with your back straight, breathe normally, and think, "It is just my perception, my mind cutting these vegetables." (This releases you from the pride of having done something.) Get used to this idea.

SOUP
- Heat oil, over medium heat, in a wok or soup pot.
- Add onion and stir occasionally, until onions are tender.
- Stir in turnips, cabbage, spinach, garlic, salt, and water; bring to a boil.
- Reduce heat to low, cover, and cook while preparing noodle dough.
- Divide noodle dough into 4 pieces.

- Roll one piece, on a well-floured board, into a thin 8-inch (20-cm) circle.
- Cut into ½-inch (1.2-cm) strips. Keep in a pile, lightly sprinkled with flour, until all are cut. (Traditionally, this is done with your hands, rolling dough into a rope, flattening it with fingers, pulling off a piece, and tossing into the soup.)
- Add remaining 4 cups (1 L) water to soup, turn heat to high, and bring to a boil.
- Stir in noodles, reduce heat to low, and cook 20 minutes or until noodles are cooked. Add more water if needed. The longer the noodles cook, the easier the soup is to digest.
- Stir in soy sauce.
- Serve in bowls and pass the chili sauce (see below).

Serves 4

CHILI SAUCE

Place the following ingredients in an electric blender or food processor and blend until smooth: 1 tablespoon chili powder, 1 teaspoon vegetable oil, 1 small green chili, ⅓ cup (75 ml) water, and a pinch salt.

3 medium leeks (500 g) cut into
  1-inch (2.5-cm) pieces (about
  4 cups)
3 medium carrots, peeled and cut
  into 1-inch (2.5-cm) pieces
  (about 3 cups)
6 medium Yukon gold or white
  potatoes (2 pounds or 1 kg),
  peeled and cut into 1-inch
  (2.5-cm) pieces (about 4 cups)
1 medium turnip, peeled and cut
  into 1-inch (2.5-cm) pieces
  (about 1 cup)
4 small shallots, peeled and
  halved
10 cups (2½ L) water
2 teaspoons sea salt
freshly ground black pepper
3 tablespoons (45 g) butter

Market-Fresh Vegetable Soup

French

One French family I know makes this thick and rich country soup, *la soupe de maman,* all year-round as the evening meal. The soup is often prepared in a pressure cooker, with enough made for several days; add soup pasta on the second day and cheese on the third. The country French are no-fuss people. The vegetables are cut on a table spread with newspaper for easy cleanup. There is nothing fancy here—just the vegetables, so their flavor can be fully appreciated. Serve with crusty country bread and fresh butter. Eat this soup like the French do: tear up pieces of bread and mix them in. To complete the meal, follow with cheese—goat, Camembert, or Comte—a yogurt, or fromage blanc topped with fruit compote.

METHOD

Mind Refresher ✿ Assemble the vegetables on a table or counter. Stand straight, relax, and breathe normally. Watch the present moment's in-and-out breaths for 30 seconds. Begin cutting vegetables.

- Put leeks, carrots, potatoes, turnip, and shallots in a large bowl, cover with water, and let soak while bringing water to a boil.
- Pour water into a soup pot, add salt and pepper, and bring to a boil over high heat.
- Discard vegetables' soaking water and stir vegetables into boiling water.
- Return to a boil, reduce heat to low, cover, and cook 45 minutes, or until vegetables are tender.
- Transfer soup and cooking liquid to an electric blender or food processor; blend to a smooth, thick mixture.
- Pour soup back into the cooking pot, stir in butter, and season with salt and pepper to taste. Heat 10 minutes over medium heat to blend flavors.

Serves 4–8 (or enough for a couple of meals)

Rice Congee with Condiments

Chinese

1 cup (200 g) uncooked rice,
  rinsed
12 cups (3 L) water
1 teaspoon sea salt
green onions, finely sliced
fresh ginger, finely grated

This all-purpose dish, sometimes called "chunk," involves cooking rice very slowly in a lot of water, with a creamy, soupy result. At breakfast it is a warming, refreshing hot cereal; at lunch a thick, nourishing soup; at supper a satisfying main dish; and at midnight an easily digested snack. A slow cooker works well for making congee. The basic ratio is one part rice to twelve parts water. Any kind of rice—white or brown, long- or short-grain, glutinous—can be used, and barley may also be substituted for rice. To make the soup even smoother, some people like to blend it after cooking. A piece of tangerine peel added to the soup while it is cooking gives it a warming quality that aids digestion. The soft consistency and bland flavor of congee can be enlivened by serving it with a variety of ingredients and condiments. It can also be poured over tender raw vegetables that have marinated for thirty minutes in soy sauce, rice wine vinegar, finely grated fresh ginger, sugar, and salt. Or it can simply be served over plain fresh spinach leaves. Congee gives strength!

METHOD

> **Mind Refresher** ✿ Prepare this recipe with the motivation to benefit others, to make them happy.

· Put rice, water, and salt in a soup pot, over high heat, and bring to a boil.
· Cover, reduce heat to low, and cook 2 hours, or until rice is very soft and has soupy consistency (brown rice will take 3–4 hours).
· Thin with water if necessary.
· Serve in bowls; garnish with green onions and ginger.
· Place condiments at center of table for each person to make a choice.

Serves 6–8

CONDIMENTS

Possible congee condiments include fresh cilantro leaves, soy sauce, chili sauce, pickled vegetables, marinated bean curd, soaked shiitake mushrooms, water chestnuts, grated carrot, or gomashio (see page 124).

1½ cups (350 g) split yellow peas

6 cups (1½ L) water

1 medium onion, peeled and
    roughly chopped (about 1 cup)

2 large sprigs fresh mint

2 tablespoons olive oil, the best
    you have

1 teaspoon sea salt

BUTTER

½ cup (125 g) butter, softened

fresh cilantro leaves (about ½ cup)

4 green onions, roughly chopped
    (about 1 cup)

4 cloves garlic, peeled

2 teaspoons ground paprika

2 teaspoons chili powder

2 teaspoons ground coriander

2 teaspoons sea salt

Yellow Split-Pea Soup with Spiced Butter
English

In the English countryside outside Cambridge is a house called the Old Vicarage, which used to be the priest's house for the church across the way. A wonderful family owns it and raised their six children there. In the summers, they rent the place to groups. The mother, father, and children do the cooking and serving. The food is always from their garden or bought from the local market or farms. The table for lunch fare is set with a large steamy bowl of soup, platters of garden-fresh salads, country bread, seasonal fruit, and a yummy dessert. This recipe is one of theirs. The creamy yellow soup is set off by a dollop of red spicy butter and served with warm pita breads. Any leftover butter can be used for topping potatoes, pasta, or tofu.

METHOD

· Pour split peas into medium bowl, cover with cold water, and soak
    overnight.
· Drain peas in colander, rinse, put into a soup pot, cover with 6 cups
    (1½ L) water, and bring to a boil over high heat.
· Stir in onion, mint, and olive oil; reduce heat to low.

> **Mind Refresher** ✿ Stand straight, breathe normally,
> and take in the aroma of the soup; concentrate on
> this aroma for 30 seconds.

· Cover and cook 1 hour or until peas are tender when crushed against
    the side of pot.
· Make butter while soup is cooking: Put all butter ingredients into
    an electric blender or food processor and blend until smooth.
    Transfer to serving bowl and chill.
· Blend soup in an electric blender or food processor until smooth.
· Return to soup pot and heat over medium heat until thickened.
· Ladle into soup bowls and stir in a generous spoonful of spiced
    butter.

Serves 4–6

Red Beet Borscht

Tajikistani, from Dauchanbe

Because Central Asia is so cold, the people rely on culinary staples that are substantial and warm. The vodka helps, but a hearty root-vegetable soup like borscht gives the body a nourishing zip. First the beets are cooked whole to make a broth. Then other vegetables are added and all are cooked to make a colorful, richly flavored soup that gets even better the next day. To make cleanup easy, chop and clean the vegetables on a newspaper; to make the job faster, chop them in a food processor.

METHOD

Mind Refresher ✿ Stand straight, breathe normally, and concentrate on your in-and-out breaths for 30 seconds. As your thoughts run here and there, keep coming back to your breath.

- Put whole beets and water into a large pot over high heat and bring to a boil.
- Reduce heat to low, cover, and cook 30 minutes.
- Heat oil in a small skillet over medium heat. Stir in onions and cook, stirring occasionally, until soft.
- Stir in tomato and cook a few more minutes.
- Add onion and tomato mix, potatoes, carrots, cabbage, bay leaf, salt, and pepper to soup pot, cover, and cook over low heat 1 hour.
- Remove cooked beets with a fork and rinse under cold water to cool. Peel and grate.
- Stir grated beets, dill, and parsley into soup; continue cooking 10 minutes to blend flavors.
- Serve garnished with sour cream or crème fraîche.

Serves 4–6

3 medium beets (500 g) whole, leaves and stems discarded
10 cups (2½ L) water
2 tablespoons olive oil or vegetable oil
1 small onion, peeled, halved, and thinly sliced (about ½ cup)
1 medium tomato, peeled and chopped (about ½ cup)
3 medium Yukon gold or white potatoes (12 ounces or 350 g), peeled and grated (about 2 cups)
2 large carrots, peeled and grated (about 1½ cups)
¼ medium-head green cabbage, finely shredded (about 4 cups)
1 bay leaf
1 teaspoon sea salt
freshly ground black pepper
3 tablespoons finely chopped fresh dill
3 tablespoons finely chopped fresh flat-leaf parsley
sour cream or crème fraîche

1 cup (200 g) dried black beans,
   picked over and rinsed
1 medium onion, peeled and
   chopped (about 1 cup)
6 cups (1½ L) water
2 medium carrots, peeled and cut
   into ½-inch (1.2-cm) pieces
   (about 2 cups)
4 medium sweet potatoes
   (2 pounds or 1 kg), peeled and
   cut into 1-inch (2.5-cm) pieces
   (about 4 cups)
1 teaspoon sea salt

SAUCE
3 tablespoons olive oil or
   vegetable oil
1 can (15 ounces or 450 g)
   crushed tomatoes
3 cloves garlic, peeled and finely
   chopped
3 tablespoons chopped fresh
   oregano or 2 teaspoons dried
   oregano
1 teaspoon ground cumin
1 teaspoon sea salt
¼ teaspoon ground cayenne, or
   to taste

Rich Black Bean Soup with Sweet Potatoes

Cuban

Black beans, sometimes called black turtle beans, are found in Mexican markets. They are used in the cuisines of Cuba as well as those of Mexico and South America. The small black beans, when cooked, make a rich dark gravy. Cubans call this soup *sopa de frijol negro* and serve it with rice and fried plantains (cooking bananas). It can also be made with red kidney beans. After eating this soup, dance a little salsa into the night.

METHOD

· Cover beans in 5 inches (12.5 cm) of water and soak overnight.
· Drain water from beans in a colander.
· Put beans, onion, and 6 cups water in a soup pot over high heat and bring to a boil.
· Reduce heat to low, cover, and cook 1 hour.

Mind Refresher ✿ Stir in ingredients with a present-moment mind.

· Stir in carrots, potatoes; cook covered 45 minutes.
· Add salt and continue cooking for 15 minutes or until beans are soft when squeezed and there is a nice rich gravy. (Adding salt in the beginning prevents the beans from cooking.)
· Make sauce while beans are cooking: Heat oil in a small skillet over medium heat. When oil is hot, add tomatoes, garlic, oregano, ground cumin, salt, and cayenne. Reduce heat to low, cover, and cook 10 minutes. Set aside.
· Stir tomato mixture into cooked beans; heat 15 minutes to blend flavors.

Serves 4–6

Shiitake Barley Tonic Soup

Chinese

The Chinese have used herbs for thousands of years to strengthen *chi*, the life force our bodies need. A good tonic soup is often served to the family each week to keep immune systems strong, building resistance to colds, flu, weakness, and disease. This hearty soup is rich, creamy, and full of flavor. Shiitake provides excellent support for the immune system. It is found dry in the Chinese food section of Asian markets. Keep a supply on hand to make the soup throughout the winter months. Astragalus root, a *chi* tonic herb resembling a large tongue depressor, is long, flat, yellowish-white, and slightly sweet tasting. It can be found in Asian markets.

METHOD

- Bring 2 cups (500 ml) water to a boil in a small saucepan, add shiitake, turn off heat, and let soak 20 minutes.
- Heat oil in a soup pot over medium-high heat. Add onions and cook, stirring occasionally, until tender.
- Add white mushrooms, barley, carrot, tomato, salt, turmeric, and cayenne; reduce heat to medium-low and cook, stirring, 5 minutes.
- Take shiitake out of water, squeeze to release excess water; reserve for soup.
- Remove stems from shiitake.

> **Mind Refresher ✿** Stand straight, breathe normally, and look at a shiitake mushroom. Concentrate on it for 30 seconds, returning to it when you catch your mind wandering.

- Slice shiitake thinly.
- Stir 10 cups (2½ L) water, shiitake mushrooms, shiitake water, and astragalus into soup pot. Turn heat to high and bring to a boil.
- Reduce heat to low, cover, and cook 1½ hours.
- Add spinach and continue cooking 15 minutes. Add more water if necessary. After sitting, soup will thicken; keep adding water to thin.
- Add soy sauce or tamari just before serving.

Serves 4–6

12 cups (3 L) water, divided: (2 cups [500 ml] and 10 cups [2½ L])

6 shiitake mushrooms

3 tablespoons olive oil or vegetable oil

1 medium onion, peeled and diced (about 1 cup)

4 ounces (70 g) white mushrooms, sliced (about 1 cup)

1 cup (250 g) whole barley

1 medium carrot, peeled and grated (about 1 cup)

1 small tomato, chopped (about ¼ cup)

1 tablespoon sea salt

½ teaspoon ground turmeric

⅛ teaspoon ground cayenne

2 sticks astragalus, optional

1 pound (500 g) fresh spinach, rinsed and coarsely chopped (about 4 cups), or 8 ounces (250 g) frozen spinach, other green leaf vegetables, or fresh nettle leaves

2 tablespoons soy sauce or tamari

4 cups (1 L) water

12 ounces (350 g) soft, medium, or firm tofu, cut into ½-inch (1.2-cm) cubes (about 1½ cups)

2 green onions, thinly sliced (about ½ cup)

4–5 tablespoons white miso, depending on saltiness

½ cup chopped fresh cilantro leaves

2 tablespoons fresh lemon juice

⅛ teaspoon ground cayenne (optional)

Lemony Miso Soup

Asian

Miso, a fermented paste made from soy beans, grain, salt, and bacteria, comes in a full range of flavors and colors. White miso, also called shiro miso or simply rice and soybean miso, has a lighter flavor than dark miso (see page 193 for more information). This light and lemony soup takes no time to make. It was served for lunch at a yoga retreat with fresh pea-and-zucchini salad, dense whole grain bread, and fresh unsalted butter. It tasted so wonderful. Try serving this soup alongside a couscous salad with garbanzo beans or a sandwich spread with hummus and topped with grilled vegetables.

METHOD

> **Mind Refresher** ✿ Make the soup with the attitude of nourishing others.

- Put water in a medium saucepan over high heat and bring to boil.
- Stir in tofu and green onions.
- Reduce heat to low and cook, uncovered, 3 minutes.
- Put miso in a small strainer, lower into soup, and push paste through strainer with a spoon until it dissolves.
- Turn off heat. Miso should not be boiled or overcooked because too much heat destroys its enzymatic properties.
- Stir in cilantro and lemon juice. Serve immediately.

Serves 4

JAPANESE MISO SOUP

INGREDIENTS: 4 cups (1 L) water, 1–2 pieces wakame seaweed (cover with hot water, soak 10 minutes or until soft, and cut into 1-inch [2.5-cm] pieces), ½ pound (250 g) firm tofu (cut into ½-inch [1.2-cm] cubes), 2 thinly sliced green onions, 3 tablespoons white or dark miso. Follow method described for Lemony Miso Soup, adding wakame at the end.

12 cups (1½ L) water

3 tablespoons olive oil

1 rounded tablespoon coarse sea salt

6 medium Yukon gold or white potatoes (1½ pounds or 750 g) (about 4 cups)

5 medium carrots (1 pound or 500 g) (about 4 cups)

1 medium turnip (about 1 cup)

1 medium tomato, cut into quarters (about 1 cup)

1 large onion, peeled, halved, and quartered (about 1½ cups)

1 pound (500 g) Italian green beans (about 2½ cups), with ends cut off and cut at an angle into ½-inch (1.2-cm) pieces

sea salt and freshly ground black pepper

Mama's Vegetable Soup

Portuguese, from Lagos

This is Mama's soup and found in most homes and restaurants. Mama makes this soup for visitors who stay at the family's youth hostel, The Rising Cock. The base is a blend of potatoes and carrots, which takes no time to cook, less than 20 minutes. Once the base has been made, vegetables can be added. Some of the choices are Italian green beans, spinach, broccoli, cauliflower, cabbage, or macaroni pasta. Mama's favorite is fresh spinach. For leftovers the first time add string beans. The second time add pasta. If there is still soup left over, add white beans and cabbage. Serve with bread.

METHOD

· Put water, olive oil, and salt into soup pot. Bring to boil.

Mind Refresher ✿ Stand straight, watch in-and-out breaths for 30 seconds.

· Peel potatoes, carrots, and turnips; halve and cut into 1½-inch (3.7-cm) quarters. Put into large bowl of water to rinse.
· Discard rinse water; add potatoes, carrots, and turnips to soup pot.
· Stir in tomato and onion, cook soup, uncovered, over medium heat for 20 minutes or until vegetables are tender.
· Cook Italian green beans or other vegetables while soup is cooking.
· Blend soup with a blender or food processor until thick and smooth. Add green beans, continuing cooking, uncovered, over medium heat until beans are tender.
· Season to taste with salt and pepper.

Serves 6–8 (or enough for a couple of meals)

A Bowl of Perceptions

Africans scoop rice with hands from bowls.
The French dunk bread in coffee bowls.
The English sip from spoons and bowls.
The Japanese slurp soup from bowls.
Asians use chopsticks with bowls.
Americans eat salads in bowls.
Greeks smash their bowls.
Monks beg with bowls.
Some lick their bowls.
Goldfish live in bowls.

Herbs and Spices for Infinite Flavors

Herbs and spices transform food, making the same basic item taste different from day to day. Potatoes, for instance, taste one way when cooked with fresh herbs and garlic, another cooked with sesame seeds, another stewed with soy sauce, another fried with mustard and cumin seeds, and, yes, still another fried with chilies. Herbs and spices also aid digestion. Some that are particularly good for this purpose are oregano, marjoram, turmeric, cumin, mint, chilies, and ginger. Every country has its favorites for transforming the taste and properties of food. Another interesting dimension of herbs and spices is their use in teas, for pleasure and for medicinal purposes.

No garden is too small for growing fresh herbs. Once picked, they can be kept in a towel in the refrigerator. When you are cooking, combine different herbs and toss them into your dishes by the handful. You can use a lot more fresh herbs than dried herbs. The more delicate herbs are good for quicker cooking methods or for adding at the last moment, while the aromatic ones are best for longer cooking methods. Combine one, two, or three from one group. Cooking with fresh herbs really makes a difference in the taste of food and makes the whole process more fun.

Here are a few seasonings from different cultures.

Flavorings

FRENCH FLAVORINGS

Fine herbs: Chives, mint, cilantro, chervil, parsley, tarragon, basil, sorrel, fennel. These fine herbs are added at the last moment. They can also be puréed with oil and kept for a year in the refrigerator. Make sure the oil covers the herbs. Scoop out the mixture as needed to add to dishes. One tablespoon or a handful equals approximately one teaspoon of dried herbs.

Aromatic herbs: Oregano, rosemary, thyme, sage, savory, bay leaf. These are best added at the beginning of cooking because they add key flavor to the food and release their flavors more slowly.

Onion, garlic, shallots: Some people have a hard time digesting these. Take the center out to make them easier to digest.

Bouquet garni: Bay leaf, celery leaves, thyme, parsley, cloves. These are used for flavoring vegetable stock and soups.

Herbes de Provence: Serpolet (wild thyme), thyme, rosemary, summer savory, marjoram, oregano, basil, fennel. These can be used to season meat and vegetable dishes.

INDIAN FLAVORINGS: Cumin seeds, fenugreek, coriander, fennel, cinnamon, cardamom, bay leaf, asafoetida, turmeric, mustard seeds (heat in oil for a few seconds first, to release flavor), garam masala (see page 192), chilies, garlic, onion, ginger.

CHINESE FLAVORINGS: Ginger, garlic, scallions, salt, sugar, cilantro, sesame seeds, Chinese five spice (anise, cinnamon, clove, fennel, and ginger—allspice or just cinnamon may be substituted), soy sauce, rice wine, sesame oil.

MEXICAN FLAVORINGS: Garlic, onion, cilantro, chilies, chili powder, oregano, cumin seed, epazote, cinnamon, cloves.

NORTH AFRICA FLAVORINGS: Cumin, saffron, cinnamon, mint, lemon, chilies, garlic, black pepper, harissa (red-pepper paste), turmeric, cardamom, clover, nutmeg.

INDONESIAN FLAVORINGS: Garlic, ginger, galangal, chilies, coconut, coriander, lemongrass, kaffir lime leaves, cumin, palm sugar, shallots, turmeric, tamarind, basil.

JAPANESE FLAVORINGS: Soy sauce, sugar, salt, green onions, ginger, miso, mirin (sweet rice wine), rice wine or sake, wasabi (horseradish), seaweeds, sesame.

THAI FLAVORINGS: Cilantro, lemongrass, galangal, chilies, kaffir lime leaf, sweet basil, ginger, tamarind, coconut milk, palm sugar.

Seaweed Varieties

BROWN ALGAE FAMILY

Kombu: Sometimes referred to as kelp, kombu is used to make a full-flavored broth for soups. Add a 6-inch (15-cm) piece to beans, vegetables, and soups. Kombu can also be marinated like pickles or baked for chips.

Wakame: Her name means "young girl," and she has a sweetish taste. Wakame must be soaked for 15 minutes and then cored before it is added to soups, stews, baked casseroles, or salads.

Nori: Mostly used for sushi, nori is also good as a snack, served in sheets alongside fried rice, or crumbled into soups, salad, grains, or steamed vegetables. Toast a sheet over a stove burner for about a minute, until it turns an iridescent green. Scoop rice onto the sheet and eat. Cats like this seaweed too—try putting some in their food.

Arame: This crisp-textured, long-stranded, nutty-tasting sea plant has a sweet flavor that is good with vegetables and grain dishes. Soak it for 15 minutes before use.

Hijiki: Often substituted for arame, hijiki is great in a vegetable salad or a couscous salad because of its pretty little strands. Some people may find this weird, but most will love the texture. Soak it for 15 minutes before use.

RED ALGAE FAMILY

Dulse: A staple in Ireland, Scotland, Wales, and parts of New England, dulse has more fiber than oat bran. Reddish-purple in color, it can be eaten raw as a snack or soaked and added to food. It goes well in salads because of its taste and color. Try adding it to a skillet with leftover potatoes and onions.

CHAPTER 3

Salads

for Watching the Mix

Wild Salad Story

Once while I was walking in the Swiss Alps, I happened to meet a very old man who had lived there his entire life. Every morning of the year, without fail, he would walk from his tiny village down by the valley stream up to the mountaintops, where he would gather the season's fare of wild roots, leaves, flowers, fruits, and nuts. On returning home, he would prepare an enormous salad and invite his neighbors to share his foraged meal.

At the time, I was living in this village, and the old man began to include me in this daily ritual. The salads were always a feast for the senses. The first bite was bitter, but once my juices were flowing, a whole spectrum of flavors—sour, salty, spicy, and sweet—came forward. The surprise of eating the same dish again and again but experiencing an infinite variety of colors, scents, textures, and tastes never failed to delight us all.

— **ANTON PINSCHOFF**, *English*

Yellow Quinoa and Corn Salad

Peruvian

1 cup (200 g) quinoa

2 cups (500 ml) water or
vegetable broth

½ cup (125 g) whole corn kernels

½ teaspoon ground turmeric

sea salt and freshly ground black
pepper

¼ medium onion, peeled and
diced (about ½ cup)

1 medium celery rib, diced (about
½ cup)

½ medium red bell pepper, diced
(about ½ cup)

½ medium red apple with skin,
diced (about 1½ cups)

1 jalapeño chili, seeded and finely
chopped

1 bunch fresh cilantro leaves,
finely chopped (about 1 cup)

½ bunch finely chopped fresh
flat-leaf parsley (about ½ cup)

This recipe is from the high and dry town of Huaraz (9,932 feet or 3,027 m), in the state of Ancash, atop the Peruvian Andes. The family who created it owned a modest-sized parcel on which they grew quinoa, potatoes, and *choclo* (a larger, moister version of hominy) and raised rabbits, chickens, and guinea pigs. Abuela, the mother and widower, was in charge of feeding seven children, plus aunts and uncles. She would go to the market, barter for vegetables, and then return home and judiciously use all the ingredients before her to provide nutritious meals for her large family. The raw vegetables were expensive but integral to the recipe, supplying much-needed moisture. The trick to making quinoa taste sweet and not bitter is to rinse the grains thoroughly to remove the naturally bitter outer coating. This recipe can be tailored to your own tastes. Try adding avocado.

METHOD

· Rinse quinoa in a fine strainer under cold water several times.
· In a large saucepan bring 4 cups (1 L) water or broth to a boil.
· Gradually stir in quinoa, corn, and turmeric (for color). Reduce heat to medium-low and cook, uncovered, stirring frequently to prevent sticking, 20 minutes or until water has evaporated.
· Pour into a medium bowl, season with salt and pepper, cover, and chill.

Mind Refresher ✿ Before chopping the vegetables, stand straight, relax, and breathe normally. Chop all vegetables and fruit with a knife of awareness.

· Mix onion, celery, red pepper, apple, chilies, cilantro, and parsley into chilled quinoa.
· Eat plain or add your favorite salad dressing.

Serves 4–6

Couscous Mint Salad

Middle Eastern and French

There are many different ways to make this salad. Couscous is coarsely ground semolina (durum wheat with the bran and germ removed) that has been precooked. Since it requires no further cooking, it's a nice grain to use as a base for different ingredient combinations. It tastes good eaten with hummus and pita bread. Or make a sandwich using pocket pita bread spread with hummus and topped with slices of grilled eggplant, couscous, lettuce, and a drizzle of yogurt.

METHOD

> **Mind Refresher ✿** Stand straight, relax, and breathe normally; mix the salad watching your mind's mix.

- Mix couscous, tomatoes, lemon juice, bell pepper, onion, parsley, mint, water, and olive oil in a large salad bowl.
- Season with salt and pepper, to taste.
- Let sit, covered, for three hours at room temperature.
- Adjust seasonings so salad is not too dry and has a light lemon flavor.

VARIATION

Orange-mint couscous: Use orange juice instead of water, and add to the other ingredients red bell pepper and raisins. For a complete meal, add garbanzo beans; a grain with beans creates complete protein.

Serves 4–6

1 cup (200 g) couscous

4 medium tomatoes (500 g), diced, with all their juice (about 4 cups)

3 fresh lemons, juiced (about ½ cup)

1 medium green bell pepper, diced (about 1 cup)

1 medium onion, diced (about 1 cup)

1 bunch flat-leaf parsley, finely chopped (about 1 cup)

½ bunch fresh mint leaves, finely chopped (about ½ cup)

¼ cup (60 ml) water

¼ cup (60 ml) olive oil

sea salt and freshly ground black pepper

Colorful Pasta Salad

Turkish

This simple pasta salad, called *coban* (meaning colorful), offers an excellent combination of textures and colors. Because there's nothing fancy about it, kids especially seem to like it. In Turkey the traditional bread, called pita, is made at home and served with every meal, as well as with yogurt as a snack. A yeasted round bread baked in a very hot oven, homemade Turkish pita is unlike the pocket bread of the same name sold in markets. In Eastern homes, a guest, whether rich or poor, is seated at an honored place at the table.

METHOD

- Cook pasta according to package directions.
- Drain and rinse with cold water; set aside 15 minutes to cool while preparing other ingredients.
- Mix pasta, beans, parsley, green pepper, lemon juice, and olive oil in a salad bowl.

> **Mind Refresher** ✿ Stand straight, breathe normally, and taste the salad; concentrate on the taste sensation in your mouth.

- Season to taste with salt and pepper.
- Serve at room temperature.
- Taste again if salad has been sitting awhile; it might need more lemon juice.

Serves 4

1 package (8 ounces or 250 g) curly fusilli noodles
1 can (15 ounces or 450 g) red kidney beans or white beans, drained
1 bunch flat-leaf parsley, finely chopped (about 1 cup)
1 medium green bell pepper, diced (about 1 cup)
¼–½ (60–125 ml) cup fresh lemon juice
¼ cup (60 ml) olive oil
sea salt and freshly ground pepper

French Vegetable Salads

French

The French like to serve just one vegetable as a salad, called an entrée, before the main course. Below is a sampling of some of the most popular ones, delicious with a slice of crusty bread to scoop up the juices. No need to be exact with measurements—the French cook by eye, taste, and feel. These dishes are served family style, on a platter or in a bowl, for everyone to help themselves.

> **Mind Refresher** ✿ Appreciate what is on the table from the season's market.

CHAMPIGNONS: SLICED MUSHROOMS
Mix fresh white mushrooms (rinsed and thinly sliced) with a squeeze of lemon juice and finely chopped fresh flat-leaf parsley; dress with heavy cream flavored with a touch of Dijon mustard and season to taste with sea salt and freshly ground black pepper.

CAROTTES RÂPÉES: GRATED CARROTS
Mix grated raw carrots and a finely chopped shallot; dress to taste with French dressing (see "Dressings," this chapter) or olive oil and lemon juice. This salad is good in winter because it's fresh, there's little else in season, and kids like it. Try it topped with sliced hard-cooked eggs.

BETTERAVES: BEETROOTS
Mix cooked beets, cut in uniform cubes, with finely chopped garlic cloves and finely chopped fresh flat-leaf parsley; dress to taste with French dressing (see "Dressings," this chapter). Beets cook very quickly in a pressure cooker. Cook up a bunch and keep them in the fridge to have ready for salads.

TOMATES: TOMATOES
Lay sliced fresh tomatoes on serving dish, sprinkle with chopped hard-boiled eggs, and drizzle with French dressing (see "Dressings," this chapter).

POMMES DE TERRE: POTATOES
Mix thinly sliced cooked potatoes with finely chopped fresh flat-leaf parsley; dress to taste with French dressing (see "Dressings," this chapter).

RADISES: RED RADISHES
Dip whole red radishes in unsalted butter and sprinkle with sea salt.

Creamy Potato Salad with Cucumber

Russian, from Belarus

Belarus, formerly called White Russia, is potato heaven; they have a recipe book with 500 ways to cook potatoes. Before the Chernobyl nuclear disaster, Russians went to this area for vacation. Now the country and the people are rebuilding. This particular potato recipe, made with potatoes, eggs, green peas, and pickling cucumbers and dressed with mayonnaise, is very simple and satisfying.

METHOD

· Put carrot in a small saucepan, with enough water to cover.
· Cover and cook until tender. Drain in a colander.
· Mix potatoes, eggs, carrot, peas, onion, and cucumbers in a medium bowl.
· Toss with mayonnaise.

> **Mind Refresher** ✿ Stand straight, taste the salad,
> and observe the taste on your tongue;
> concentrate on it for 30 seconds.

· Season to taste with salt and pepper.
· Chill until serving time.

Serves 4–6

1 small carrot, peeled and diced (about ½ cup)
5 medium Yukon or white potatoes (1½ pounds or 750 g), cooked, peeled, and cut into ½-inch (1.2-cm) pieces (about 3 cups)
2 hard-cooked large eggs, finely chopped
1 cup (250 g) green peas, cooked
1 small onion, finely chopped (about ½ cup)
2 fresh pickling cucumbers, peeled and diced, or dill pickles (about ½ cup)
3 tablespoons mayonnaise
sea salt and freshly ground black pepper

6 (4-inch or 10-cm) pieces
    wakame
2 ounces (60 g) vermicelli rice
    noodles
1 medium cucumber, peeled,
    halved, seeded, and thinly
    sliced (about 1½ cups)
lettuce leaves

DRESSING
1 tablespoon white sesame seeds
1 tablespoon soy sauce
1 tablespoon rice vinegar
1 teaspoon sesame oil
1 teaspoon mirin, sake, or lemon
    juice with a touch of honey
pinch ground cayenne

Sea-Fresh Wakame Salad
Japanese

The Japanese have always eaten seaweeds in their cuisine, but except
for sushi they are a new taste for most people. They work well in soups
and salads. It is easier to use them if you think of them as just another
vegetable. Toss them into salads using tomatoes, onion, avocadoes,
cilantro, and green chilies. Very good seaweed is harvested in Japan
as well as on the coasts of Oregon, Maine, New Zealand, Brittany, and
Ireland. Packaged seaweeds can be found in natural food stores and
Asian markets. See page 193 for more information.

METHOD

· Cover wakame in a small bowl with boiling-hot water, 10 minutes, or
    until soft.
· Cover noodles in another small bowl with boiling-hot water, 10
    minutes, or until soft.
· Drain off noodle water, squeeze out moisture from noodles, and
    coarsely chop.
· Drain off wakame water, squeeze out moisture from wakame, remove
    center rib, and cut into 1-inch (2.5-cm) pieces (about ½ cup)
· Mix noodles, wakame, and cucumber in a medium bowl.

> **Mind Refresher** ✿ Stand straight, breathe normally,
> and watch your breath for 30 seconds.

· Make dressing: Roast sesame seeds in a small skillet, over high heat,
    shaking pan, until lightly brown. Put 2 teaspoons of seeds into
    mortar or coffee grinder and grind to a powder to release flavor.
    Pour into a small bowl and stir in soy sauce, rice vinegar, sesame
    oil, mirin, and cayenne.
· Toss noodles with dressing.
· Arrange lettuce leaves on a serving plate and place noodle mixture in
    a mound on top.
· Sprinkle with remaining sesame seeds.

Serves 4

All the Goodies Green Salad

North American, from California

This big tossed green salad features an interesting combination of flavors and textures. Add to bitter arugula and romaine lettuce sweet dates and corn, crunchy croutons, lush avocado, and tangy tomatoes, all topped with goat cheese and sunflower seeds, and you have a salad that truly offers all the goodies. Serve it in a big bowl on the table. Arugula is a bitter green available in most supermarkets today; if you can't find it, use another type of lettuce.

METHOD

> **Mind Refresher** ✿ Stand straight, breathe normally, and watch the mind for 30 seconds.

· Mix romaine lettuce, arugula, corn, dates, croutons, green onions, avocado, and tomato together in a large salad bowl.
· Toss with balsamic vinegar dressing to taste.
· Sprinkle cheese and seeds on top.

Serves 4

1 head romaine lettuce, rinsed and torn into bite-size pieces
½ cup (60 g) arugula, rinsed
1 cup (250 g) whole corn kernels
½ cup (125 g) dates, pitted and chopped
2 cups (90 g) bite-sized croutons
2 green onions, thinly sliced (about ½ cup)
1 medium avocado, stone removed, peeled and cubed
1 medium tomato, diced (about ½ cup)
balsamic vinegar dressing (see "Dressings," this chapter)
½ cup (60 g) goat or feta cheese, crumbled
¼ cup (45 g) sunflower seeds

4 medium navel oranges
2 medium lemons
1 small red onion, thinly sliced
3 tablespoons (approximately)
    extra virgin olive oil
sea salt and freshly ground black
    pepper
2 tablespoons finely chopped
    fresh mint or basil leaves

Olive Oil and Mint Orange Salad

Italian

Sicilians often eat this *insalata* with good crusty bread and a glass of white wine. The oranges and lemons are drizzled with just a little olive oil and then allowed to sit, making a wonderful sauce for scooping up with bread. Try leaving out the lemons for a less tart flavor, or use the popular Meyer lemon, which has the flavor and aroma of sweet lime, lemon, and Mandarin orange. This salad goes well with polenta and spicy food.

METHOD

· Peel oranges and lemons so none of the bitter white under-skin
    is left.
· Slice into rounds, ¼ inch (6 mm) thick.

> **Mind Refresher** ✿ Stand straight, breathe normally,
> and observe the aroma and color of the oranges;
> concentrate on these sensations for 30 seconds.

· Arrange oranges, lemons, and onions alternately on a platter.
· Drizzle oil over fruit to glaze, season with salt and pepper, and
    sprinkle with mint or basil.
· Let stand 2 hours, covered at room temperature, so juices can mingle.
· Serve at room temperature.

Crunchy Taco Salad

North American, from the Southwest

This big meal salad is loaded with beans, chilies, tomatoes, cheese, and tortilla chips and tossed with a creamy, spicy guacamole dressing. With all these flavors and textures, this salad is sure to satisfy your taste buds. In the Southwest, Mexican food is the most popular cuisine. A bag of tortilla chips and a jar of salsa are basic staples found in everyone's refrigerators and cupboards.

METHOD

- Mix, cabbage, tomatoes, onions, bell pepper, beans, corn and chili powder in a salad bowl.

> **Mind Refresher ✿** Stand straight, breathe normally, and watch the breath as you toss the salad.

- Toss salad with guacamole dressing; let salad sit 10 minutes.
- Sprinkle with cheese and tortilla chips and serve.
- Pass extra dressing.

Serves 4

1 small head green cabbage, thinly sliced (about 4 cups), or lettuce

2 medium tomatoes, diced (about 1 cup)

1 small onion, diced (about ½ cup)

1 medium green bell pepper, diced (about 1 cup)

1 can (15 ounces or 450 g) kidney, pinto, or black beans, drained

1 can (8 ounces or 250 g) whole corn kernels

½ teaspoon chili powder

½–1 cup (125–250 g) guacamole dressing (see "Dressings," in this chapter)

½ cup (60 g) feta cheese, crumbled, or cheddar cheese, shredded

2 cups (125 g) corn tortilla chips, crumbled

2 medium red bell peppers

2 medium green bell peppers

3 tablespoons olive oil

2 cans (29 ounces or 870 g) diced
tomatoes, drained, or 6 fresh
tomatoes, peeled

4–6 cloves garlic, peeled, mashed
and finely chopped

sea salt and freshly ground black
pepper

½ bunch fresh flat-leaf parsley
or cilantro leaves, finely
chopped (about ½ cup)

Roasted Red Pepper and Garlic Salad

Israeli and French

This colorful salad is full of garlic for you garlic lovers. Cooked first, then left to marinate before serving, it goes well with bread to scoop up the juices. To mash the garlic, crush each clove lightly with a knife (this releases the skin), peel, place the blade of a heavy knife on the clove, and smash down and forward to crush it to a pulp. The crushing releases essential oils and makes the garlic easier to chop to a puree. The recipe calls for flat-leaf parsley or fresh cilantro; I prefer using cilantro because it lifts the flavor, giving the dish a fresh taste.

METHOD

· Place peppers directly on the stove flame or under a broiler in the oven until charred on all sides.
· Put peppers in a plastic bag to sweat for 15 minutes.
· Take off charred skins under running water.
· Remove core, seeds, and white veins.

> **Mind Refresher** ❖ Stand straight, breathe normally, and watch your in-and-out breaths while slicing the peppers—nothing else to do.

· Thinly slice peppers lengthwise into ¼-inch (6-mm) strips.
· Heat oil in a skillet, over medium heat; stir in peppers, tomatoes, and garlic; cook and stir, uncovered, for 5 minutes, until flavors are blended.
· Season to taste with salt and pepper.
· Refrigerate until serving time.
· Stir in parsley or cilantro and serve with crusty bread.

Serves 4

〜〜〜〜〜〜〜〜〜

½ cup (250 ml) water
¼ cup (60 ml) fresh lemon juice
¼ medium onion, peeled
1 medium avocado, peeled, stone
removed, and quartered
1 clove garlic, peeled
1 fresh serrano green chili pepper
generous handful fresh cilantro
leaves (about ¼ cup)
2 tablespoons olive oil or
vegetable oil
1 teaspoon sea salt

Spicy Guacamole Dressing

North American, from Texas

This dressing is creamy and smooth, with the flavors of garlic, chili, and lemon juice. It is suitable for the taco salad or as a dip for fresh raw vegetables. Feel free to spice it up. Try the addition of sun-dried tomatoes.

METHOD

Mind Refresher ❂ **Stand straight, breathe normally, and watch the mix of the mind for 30 seconds.**

· In an electric blender or food processor, blend water, lemon juice, onion, avocado, garlic, chili, cilantro leaves, oil, and salt until smooth and creamy. Add more water if too thick.

Makes 1 cup (250 g)

1 tablespoon good strong red wine
vinegar or cider vinegar
½–1 teaspoon Dijon mustard
(optional)
¼ teaspoon sea salt
freshly ground black pepper
4–5 tablespoons vegetable oil or
other flavored oil
optional: finely chopped garlic,
finely chopped shallot, or
1 tablespoon fresh herbs,
such as basil, dill, fennel,
winter savory, thyme, rosemary,
or oregano

Classic French Dressing

French

To save time in salad making, mix your dressing in the bottom of the salad bowl, put your lettuce on top, and at serving time toss the salad. This is a French tip.

METHOD

· Mix vinegar, mustard, salt, and pepper in a small mixing bowl.

Mind Refresher ❂ **Stand straight, breathe normally, and concentrate on your breath as you blend in the oil.**

· With a fork, slowly mix in oil until blended.
· Add optional ingredients, if desired.

Makes ⅓ cup (75 ml)

Balsamic Vinegar Dressing

North American, from California

2 tablespoons balsamic vinegar
1 tablespoon red wine vinegar
1 teaspoon granulated sugar
¼ teaspoon dried oregano or
   1 teaspoon fresh oregano
1 small clove garlic, finely
   chopped
3 tablespoons olive oil or
   vegetable oil
sea salt and freshly ground black
   pepper

Balsamic vinegar gives dressing a good sweet earthy quality. A garden salad made with candied walnuts, blue cheese, and sliced apples, then tossed with balsamic dressing, is yummy.

METHOD

· Mix vinegars, sugar, oregano, and garlic in a small bowl.

> **Mind Refresher** ✿ **Stand straight, breathe normally, and rest your mind on the aromas for 30 seconds.**

· With a fork, slowly mix in oil until blended.
· Season with salt and pepper.

Makes ⅓ cup (75 ml)

Creamy Tahini Dressing

English

2 tablespoons lemon juice or
   vinegar
1 teaspoon soy sauce or tamari
1 teaspoon honey
½ teaspoon finely chopped clove
   garlic or fresh ginger root
pinch ground cayenne
2 tablespoons tahini
1 teaspoon olive oil
1 tablespoon water to thin

A dressing made with tahini, or sesame paste, not only gives a delicious hearty flavor to fresh vegetable salads but also adds protein. Toss this dressing with baby potatoes, fresh spinach leaves, sliced red onion, and a sprinkle of sesame seeds for an easy meal. Try adding Dijon mustard to dressing mix.

METHOD

· Mix lemon or vinegar, soy, and honey in a small bowl.

> **Mind Refresher** ✿ **Stand straight, breathe normally, and watch your breaths as you mix in the tahini and oil.**

· With a fork, slowly mix in tahini and oil until blended.
· Thin with water until consistency is that of heavy cream.

Makes ⅓ cup (75 ml)

Making a Salad Dressing and Salad

You are in the kitchen beginning to make a French salad dressing. In walks your sister and says, "You're going to make it like that? That's not the way. You must first put the salt in and then the vinegar. That is the way." She fears the dressing will not taste good if you do not do it her way. This is her fixed idea. You start to become angry and hurt, but you catch yourself. You were going to add the vinegar, salt, and mustard at the same time and then the oil. This way was fine for you, but OK, this time you will try her way. You don't have to feel wrong about your way. No big deal. You can be flexible and open-minded. This time you do it differently.

The struggles that happen in our minds when making a simple dressing and salad: doubt and fear that we won't make it right; the expectation that it will be perfect, our idea of what is perfect; the hope others will praise you for making a perfect salad; the hurt when no one says anything positive or someone criticizes you; the pride of thinking you know the best way; the desire to be famous for making the best salad. Remember your thirty seconds of Fresh Mind meditation! Afterward, continue making your dressing and salad choices, and appreciate whatever happens.

CUTTING VEGETABLES
Vegetables cut into different shapes add variety to dishes. Depending on the vegetable, it may be julienned, minced, chopped, cubed, shaved, sliced, or diced; possible shapes include squares, matchsticks, irregular chunks, crescents, flowers, rounds, half-rounds, and quarter-rounds.

Dijon mustard or no mustard
First salt then vinegar
Everything mixed at once
Salad dressing on bottom, lettuce on top
Toss the dressing and lettuce at serving time
Pour oil and vinegar on top of lettuce
Type of vinegar: store-bought, homemade, balsamic, strawberry, raspberry, or cider
Kind of oil: olive, walnut, or safflower
Kind of lettuce: romaine, butter, iceberg, or gourmet blend
Rock salt or fine salt
Pepper or no pepper

Violà! Finished! The salad is perfect because you were in the moment.

CHAPTER 4

Main Dishes

for Serving Compassion

The Crab Story

I was born and raised in Brittany, on the seaside. A popular local dish is live crabs, which we would buy at market to be sure they were fresh. To cook the crabs, you throw them in boiling water for some minutes. The dish is delicious warm or cold with vinaigrette, spicy mayonnaise, or simply au naturel.

When I was fifty-five years old, I moved with my wife back to Brittany, to a small seaside village. After eighteen months, our neighbor, a fisherman, offered me small live crabs for dinner. I was proud of this first sign of friendship and went triumphantly home, looking forward to my crab dinner. I forgot that my wife is a Buddhist; she was quite against the assassination I had in mind. So I waited for nightfall to send the crabs back to the ocean, hoping my neighbor wouldn't see me with my bucket.

The ordeal was not finished. About five hours later I went shopping alone for dinner. My desire for crabs was so deep after this frustration that I could not resist buying some live crabs, which in my deluded state I hoped to sneak into the house and prepare without my wife's knowledge. I was in the kitchen when she walked in and saw the crabs. In exasperation, she exclaimed, "What are you doing?" She looked like she was ready to kill me, but instead she stormed out of the house.

We did not see her for one whole day. When she returned home, the family gathered on the front lawn to welcome her. At that very moment another neighbor came by with a box full of live crabs. We kindly thanked the fisherman. After he left, we all burst out laughing. My wife took the crabs to the ocean that evening, and no crabs were ever cooked in our house.

DANIEL DENIS, *French*

Buttery Crisp Potato Cake

French, from Brittany's Vannes

Brittany is a region in the northwest corner of France with chilly sea weather, so potatoes and other hearty foods are extremely popular there. The local potatoes are buttery yellow, but any potato will do for this recipe; even sweet potatoes would be excellent. This dish, *galette de pommes de terre,* not only looks especially pretty but also is a good way to use up leftover potatoes. It is simple to make, and the potato mixture can be prepared ahead of time. Serve this light golden brown cake with an artichoke or steamed vegetables and mustard.

5 large Yukon gold or white potatoes (2½ pounds or 1¼ kg), unpeeled and cooked

2 cups (300 g) all-purpose flour

1 cup (8 ounces or 250 g) butter, melted

1½ teaspoons sea salt

¼ teaspoon freshly ground black pepper

1 egg yolk, beaten

METHOD

- Preheat oven to 425° F (220° C).
- Mash potatoes in a medium bowl with a fork to make about 4 cups.
- Mix in flour, butter, salt, and pepper.
- On an ungreased cookie sheet, shape potato mixture into a 9-inch (22.5-cm) circle, ½ inch (1.2 cm) thick.
- Brush egg yolk on top (the egg makes a brown glaze), using a brush or your fingertips.
- Bake 35–40 minutes or until golden brown and firm to touch.
- Transfer to a serving plate and cut into wedges at the table.

Mind Refresher ❂ Serve with loving kindness.

Serves 6

4 large tomatoes (2 pounds or
    1 kg)
3 tablespoons olive oil
8 medium Yukon gold or white
    potatoes (3 pounds or 1½ kg),
    peeled, halved, and sliced
½ cup (125 g) red lentils, rinsed
2–3 small fresh green chilies,
    seeded and thinly sliced
    lengthwise
1 cup (250 ml) water
2 teaspoons sea salt
8 slices melting cheese, such as
    fontina, Cantal, or Monterey
    Jack
fresh flat-leaf parsley

Red Creamy Stewed Potatoes

Bhutanese

This recipe uses red lentils, which are extremely quick to cook and tend to lose their red color during cooking. They do not need to be soaked first, just cooked for about twenty minutes. Note that after being washed, the lentils sometimes look soapy; don't worry—this is only the starch being released. Red lentils make a nice gravy for the potatoes and for other dishes as well. You will find the gravy has lots of flavor with just chilies and no onions or garlic (in retreat situations, for better practice results, onion and garlic are not used—they are said to make the mind sleepy). Try this recipe with a green salad dressed with mustard vinaigrette and grilled portabella mushrooms.

METHOD

· Put tomatoes into boiling water for 1 minute to loosen skin; take out with a fork and peel.

> **Mind Refresher ✿** Stand straight and watch your in-and-out breaths as you chop tomatoes.

· Roughly chop tomatoes (about 3 cups) and set aside.
· Heat olive oil in a 2-quart (2-L) heavy casserole over medium-high heat.
· Stir in tomatoes; cook and stir 1 minute.
· Add potatoes, reduce heat to medium-low, stir occasionally, and cook 3 minutes to release flavors.
· Mix in lentils, chilies, water, and salt; bring to a boil over high heat.
· Reduce heat to low and simmer potatoes, covered, stirring occasionally, 40 minutes or until a thick sauce develops and potatoes are cooked through.
· Watch that the mixture does not stick to the casserole during cooking; if it does, add more water.
· At serving time, place slices of cheese over hot potatoes, sprinkle with parsley, and cover; the cheese will melt on the way to the table.

Serves 4–6

Potato and Egg Tortilla

Spanish, from Santillana Village

½ cup olive oil

5 large Yukon gold or white potatoes (2½ pounds or 1¼ kg), peeled and thinly sliced

1 medium onion, peeled, halved, and thinly sliced (about 1 cup)

4 large eggs

1 teaspoon sea salt

¼ teaspoon freshly ground black pepper

olive oil

This flat round egg cake with potatoes and caramelized onions offers a very different texture from the French galette in the previous recipe. The Spanish eat this cake for dinner at ten o'clock at night. They also take it for picnics and eat it between two pieces of bread like a sandwich. For lunch or dinner it is served with a salad, bread, and red wine, followed by a salad with manchego cheese.

METHOD

· Heat oil in a 10-inch (25-cm) nonstick skillet, over medium heat.
· Stir in potatoes and onions; cook, uncovered, stirring occasionally, 30 minutes or until potatoes and onions are brown, tender, and caramelized.

Mind Refresher ❂ Beat out the mind's poisons as you beat eggs.

· Beat eggs, salt, and pepper in a medium bowl.
· Mix potatoes and onions with eggs; pour back into skillet and cook over medium heat, using a spatula to push sides of mixture toward center to form a firm round cake.
· Turn potato cake over by inverting it onto a plate the size of the pan, then sliding it back into the pan to continue cooking on the other side, until brown and firm. Continue pushing sides with spatula to form cake.
· Slide tortilla onto a serving plate and brush with a little olive oil.

Serves 4

VARIATIONS

Consider these two non-potato tortilla variations:

Zucchini and onion: Cook finely chopped zucchini with onion until soft. Add finely chopped fresh flat-leaf parsley and a clove of garlic. Stir in eggs, salt, and pepper. Cook as above.

Artichoke and onion: Cook finely chopped artichoke hearts with onion until soft. Add finely chopped fresh flat-leaf parsley and a clove of garlic. Stir in eggs, salt, and pepper. Cook as above.

5 large Yukon gold or white
    potatoes (2½ pounds or
    1¼ kg), peeled
1 tablespoon butter (for buttering
    baking dish)
½ clove garlic, peeled
⅓ cup (75 g) melted butter
sea salt and freshly ground black
    pepper
2 cups (500 ml) half-and-half
⅛ teaspoon ground nutmeg
1 cup (125 g) shredded Gruyère
    cheese, optional

Grandmere's Crusty Gratin Potatoes

French

The potato is a favorite in France, as it is in many European countries;
a meal is not a meal to a Frenchman without potatoes and bread. The
buttery yellow potatoes in Brittany are typically used, but any local
potato will be good for this recipe. A gratin is a baked dish with a crusty
top. The potatoes are baked in milk, giving the finished dish a rich
golden brown top and a creamy interior. Serve with a green salad.

METHOD

· Preheat oven to 325° F (160° C).

> **Mind Refresher** ✿ Stand straight, breathe normally,
> and cut potatoes with a knife of awareness.

· Cut potatoes into very thin slices (¹⁄₁₆ inch or 2 mm).
· Rinse potatoes and lay them on paper towels to dry.
· Butter a 9 x 9 x 2–inch (23 x 23 x 5–cm) baking pan and rub
    generously with garlic clove.
· Layer a third of potatoes and a third of melted butter in baking dish.
    Season with salt and pepper.
· Repeat layers until all potatoes are used.
· Mix half-and-half with nutmeg in a small bowl. Pour over potatoes.
· Sprinkle with cheese, if desired.
· Bake, uncovered, 1½ hours or until rich dark-golden crust develops.

Serves 4

VARIATIONS

Add green chili strips between the potato layers.

Add cooked and sliced chestnuts between the potato layers.

Mix and Match with Baked Potatoes

North American

Everyone seems to love a baked potato. It is no-thinking cooking. Just put the potatoes in the oven and go do something else. Come back in an hour and put the meal together by mixing and matching your toppings. This recipe was recommended by college students as one of their standby meals.

METHOD

- Preheat oven to 400° F (200° C).
- Wash and scrub potatoes well; dry and prick in several places with a fork.
- Place potatoes directly on oven rack.

> **Mind Refresher ❁** Relax and breathe normally;
> as potatoes bake, think,
> "May all the anger in the world bake away."

- Bake 1 hour or until the flesh gives and feels soft.
- Split potatoes and press all around outside with fingertips to loosen pulp.
- Now mix and match.
- Cook the vegetables of your choice: Heat oil in a medium skillet over medium heat, add fresh bite-sized vegetables, and cook, stirring occasionally, until tender. Use frozen vegetables to make this step even quicker and easier.
- Place baked potatoes on a serving plate. Fill with vegetables and top with the sauce and garnish of your choice.
- Serve with a salad for a complete meal.

Serves 4

MORE BAKED POTATO SAUCE SUGGESTIONS

Herb butter: Mix together finely chopped fresh chives, tarragon, thyme, and parsley, a squeeze of lemon juice, a little finely chopped onion, a pinch of black pepper, and ¼ cup (60 g) softened butter. Make a paste and store in refrigerator.

Thousand Island sauce: Mix together mayonnaise, finely chopped tomato, thinly sliced green onion, a dash Worcestershire sauce, and salt and pepper.

4 Idaho baking potatoes, other large potatoes, or sweet potatoes

VEGETABLE SUGGESTIONS
Try one or more of these: green bell peppers, zucchini, peas, onions, broccoli, mushrooms, cauliflower, tomatoes, carrots, or chilies.

SAUCE SUGGESTIONS
Try one or more of these: yogurt, sour cream, ranch dressing, herb butter, spaghetti sauce, curry sauce, barbecue sauce, tahini sauce, pesto sauce, tomato salsa, guacamole sauce, cottage cheese, shredded cheese, chili beans, refried beans, or lentils.

GARNISH SUGGESTIONS
Try one or more of these: gomashio (sea salt and toasted sesame seeds; see page 124), tamari, roasted sunflower seeds, sesame seeds, or green onions.

1 cup (200 g) short-grain brown
    rice
2 cups (500 ml) water
¼ teaspoon sea salt

Classic Macrobiotic Brown Rice

Japanese

The macrobiotic movement in the sixties taught everyone about the nutritional value and hearty nutty flavor of brown rice. Rice comes in three grain sizes: short, medium, and long. The short and medium grains grow in temperate areas while the long-grain varieties grow in the tropics. In hotter weather, long-grain rice is preferred. Brown rice is very strengthening and nourishing to the body's vital energy. Because it is chewier than white rice, it takes some getting used to. To make digestion easier, soak the rice overnight or for at least an hour. The Japanese use salt in the cooking because they believe it is alkaline-forming and so balances the acid-forming grains. Dry roasting the rice before cooking it imparts a nuttier flavor. The secret to good brown rice is to cook it in a pot approximately the size of the portion you are making. A simple bowl of brown rice tastes great with tamari and nutritional yeast or a drizzle of olive oil, a squeeze of lemon juice, and a sprinkle of fresh herbs.

METHOD

· Rinse rice: In a medium bowl, cover rice with water, stir with your hand a couple times, drain off water, and repeat two more times or until water runs clear.
· Mix rice, cooking water, and salt in a 1-quart (1-L) saucepan and bring to a boil over high heat.
· Reduce heat to low, cover with a tight-fitting lid, and cook 1 hour or until the surface of the rice has little craters where steam has escaped and there is no more water. A flame tamer may be used to prevent burning.
· Let sit 5 minutes, covered, before serving.

Mind Refresher ✿ Offer rice while visualizing that it multiplies to fill all of space and that all beings have causes and conditions to have food.

Makes 3½ cups (850 g)

Roasted: Heat uncooked rice in dry cast-iron skillet over medium heat 2 minutes or until light brown and fragrant. Add rice to boiling water and cook as above. Keep any reserve dry-roasted rice in a jar to use for rice cream cereal, which is made as follows: Grind rice in a coffee grinder. Stir 1 cup (200 g) ground rice into 2 cups (500 ml) boiling water, cover, and cook over low heat 10 minutes or until consistency is creamy.

Pressure-cooked: This process makes brown rice easier to digest. Use 4 cups rice to 5 cups (1¼ L) water, and add ¼ teaspoon sea salt for a 4–6-quart (1½-L) pressure cooker. Presoak rice if desired; it will taste better if presoaked. Bring to full pressure, then slip a flame tamer under the cooker, reduce heat to low, and cook 45 minutes.

7-ounce (200-g) cake firm tofu
    (half a 14-ounce or 400-g cake)
1 tablespoon dark soy sauce
1 tablespoon light soy sauce
1 tablespoon water
1 tablespoon finely chopped
    fresh ginger
pinch granulated sugar
2 tablespoons toasted sesame oil
1 green onion, cut diagonally into
    1-inch (2.5-cm) pieces
2 tablespoons chopped fresh
    cilantro leaves

Steamed Tofu Sauced with Soy and Cilantro

Chinese from Hong Kong

This recipe is easy and delicious. Tofu is made from soybeans, which are very rich in protein but difficult to digest. The Chinese have long known this, so they rarely cook with the whole beans. They prefer tofu (which comes firm, soft, or silky), soymilk, and fermented products such as tempeh, miso, shoyu (soy sauce), and tamari. Another variety of soy sauce can be substituted for the light and dark soy sauces in this recipe. The toasted sesame oil adds a very aromatic touch. Serve with rice and two other vegetable dishes, as the Chinese do.

METHOD

· Steam tofu cake in a sieve over boiling water, covered, 5 minutes or until soft.

> **Mind Refresher** ✿ Watch the present-moment mind for 30 seconds.

· Heat soy sauces, water, ginger, and sugar in a small saucepan over medium heat.
· Place cooked tofu on a serving dish.
· Pour hot soy sauce over tofu, drizzle with sesame oil, and garnish with green onions and coriander leaves.
· Serve immediately to keep tofu soft, with rice.

Serves 2–4 (small portions)

GARNISH VARIATION
Garnish with English cucumber, seeded and cut in julienne strips, and a pinch of Szechwan pepper.

Tofu and Vegetables in Creamy Sesame Sauce

Korean

Tahini is a paste made from ground hulled sesame seeds. Similar to peanut butter, this nutritious spread complements vegetables. It is very versatile; use it like butter on your toast, in salad dressings, in soups, and in desserts. Here it makes a delicious sauce for the bland tofu.

METHOD

> **Mind Refresher** ✿ Before beginning to cook, stand straight, relax, and breathe normally; watch your breath for 30 seconds.

· Heat 2 tablespoons oil in a large nonstick skillet over medium high heat.
· Stir in tofu and cook until lightly browned. Remove tofu from skillet and set aside.
· Add remaining 2 tablespoons of oil to skillet. Cook onions over medium heat, stirring occasionally, 10 minutes or until soft.
· Stir in garlic, chili, ginger, carrot, and zucchini. Continue cooking 3 minutes, stirring occasionally.
· Make sauce: Mix boiling water, tahini, soy sauce, and honey in a small bowl.
· Pour sauce along with tofu pieces into skillet, reduce heat to low, cover, and cook, stirring occasionally, 15 minutes or until vegetables are tender. Add more water if too thick or there is not enough sauce.
· Transfer to a serving dish and garnish with sesame seeds and chopped cucumber. Serve with rice or noodles.

Serves 4–6

4 tablespoons vegetable oil (2 tablespoons and 2 tablespoons)
1 package (14 ounces or 400 g) firm tofu, patted dry with a towel, halved, and cut into ¾-inch (2-cm) pieces
1 medium onion, peeled, halved, and finely sliced (about 1 cup)
2 cloves garlic, peeled and finely chopped
1 small fresh red or green chili, finely chopped
¼ teaspoon finely chopped fresh ginger
2 medium carrots, peeled and cut into thin, matchlike sticks (about 2 cups)
2 medium zucchini, cut into thin, matchlike sticks (about 2 cups)

SAUCE
1 cup (250 ml) boiling water
½ cup (125 g) tahini
4 teaspoons soy sauce
4 teaspoons honey
1 tablespoon sesame seeds
½ cup (125 g) diced, peeled, and seeded cucumber

5 tablespoons vegetable oil
  (3 tablespoons and 2
  tablespoons)
3 cloves garlic, peeled and finely
  chopped
7 ounces (200 g) extra-firm
  tofu (half a 14-ounce or 400-g
  package), towel dried and cut
  into ¾-inch (2-cm) pieces
1 medium onion, peeled, halved,
  and sliced into ¼-inch slices
  (about 1 cup)
2 English cucumbers, peeled,
  quartered lengthwise, and
  cut into 1-inch (2.5-cm) pieces
  (about 3 cups)
1 can (8 ounces or 250 g) sliced
  pineapple in juice, drained
  and cut into ½-inch (1.2-cm)
  pieces (about 1 cup)
2 medium tomatoes, cut into
  ½-inch (1.2-cm) wedges (about
  1 cup)
1 teaspoon sea salt
1 teaspoon granulated sugar
1–2 tablespoons Thai chili sauce
  or ketchup
1 teaspoon soy sauce
¼ cup (60 ml) water
½ cup fresh cilantro leaves

Sweet and Sour Stir-Fried Vegetables

Thai

This recipe is served at the Jamjuree Thai Kitchen in Yangon, the capital of Myanmar (formerly Burma). The restaurant sits facing a huge pagoda shimmering with gold and holding relics of Buddha. Now that the country's borders are open, people from all over come to visit this holy site. At the restaurant they order vegetarian dishes like the one described here. Prepared with cucumbers and pineapple, it has a delightful, light sweet-and-sour flavor. The secret to effortless Thai cooking is advance preparation—having all the vegetables chopped, cut, or cubed ahead of time. Family meals are made with an easy stir-fry, rice, salad, and fruit.

METHOD

> **Mind Refresher** ✿ Before preparing the vegetables, arrange them in front of you. Stand straight, breathe normally, and watch the moment's breath for 30 seconds.

- Heat 3 tablespoons oil in a wok or large nonstick skillet over medium-high heat.
- Stir in garlic and heat 30 seconds or until fragrant, not burned.
- Stir in tofu and cook, stirring occasionally, about 10 minutes, until golden brown; remove tofu from skillet and set aside.
- Heat 2 tablespoons oil in skillet over medium heat; add onion and cook, stirring occasionally, until tender.
- Stir in cucumbers and pineapple; cook, stirring, 2 minutes.
- Add tomatoes, salt, sugar, chili sauce, and soy sauce, cover, reduce heat to medium, and cook, stirring occasionally, until vegetables are tender.
- Stir in water and tofu, heat a few minutes more.
- Stir cilantro leaves and serve with rice.

Serves 4

2 tablespoons vegetable oil or
    sesame oil
1 medium onion, peeled, halved,
    and thinly sliced (about 1 cup)
6 cups (750 g) vegetables;
    combination of three, such as
    snap peas, sliced mushrooms,
    and carrots or cabbage,
    broccoli, and zucchini

FLAVORING MIXTURE
½ cup (125 ml) fresh lemon juice
    (about 3 lemons)
¼ cup (60 g) honey
¼ cup (60 ml) tamari
2 tablespoon grated fresh
    ginger root
½ teaspoon sea salt

Ginger-Lemon Stir-Fried Vegetables

Australian

This recipe provides an easy one-pot formula for making all kinds
of delicious vegetable meals. By going to the market and seeing
what catches your eye that day—based on color, texture, freshness,
and price—you can create many colorful and interesting dishes. In
Australia the vegetables are so fresh and beautiful that it is hard not
to be inspired. This dish shows the influence of Asian cultures on
Australians' home cooking.

METHOD

· Cut vegetables into different shapes for texture: slices, circles,
    diagonals. Wash and drain separately; set aside.

> **Mind Refresher** ✿ Stand straight, breath normally,
> and look at one piece of cut vegetable;
> concentrate on it for 30 seconds.

· Make flavoring mixture: mix lemon juice, honey, tamari, ginger, and
    salt in a small bowl until blended; set aside.
· Heat oil in a Chinese wok or medium skillet over medium-high heat.
· Add onion and cook, stirring occasionally, 3 minutes or until tender.
· Mix in sturdier vegetables; cook and stir a few minutes to soften
    slightly.
· Add remaining vegetables and flavoring mixture, reduce heat to low,
    and cover. Let vegetables steam in their own juices 5 minutes or
    until they are tender but still crisp.
· Serve with rice or potatoes.

Serves 4

VARIATIONS
Instead of serving this dish with rice or potatoes, toss it with cooked
noodles—soba, rice, or egg. For protein and texture, add cooked tofu.
For an Italian flavor, use sun-dried tomatoes, zucchini, and eggplant.

Lightly Battered Fried Vegetables

Japanese

This is a fun dish to serve. Choosing from the current season's vegetables allows for a variety of tastes. The vegetables are deep-fried in batter until crisp, with their freshness protected. Serve them on a platter with a dipping sauce of soy sauce and grated ginger, accompanied by a bowl of rice or noodles sprinkled with sesame seeds. The Japanese use short-grain rice. I got this recipe from a friend, whose parents used to serve it at the family's Tokyo restaurant.

METHOD

> **Mind Refresher** ✿ Stand straight, breathe normally, and concentrate on the in-and-out breaths for 30 seconds.

- Prepare vegetables and set aside.
- Heat oil in a deep pot, over high heat, to 320° F (160° C).
- Make batter: Beat egg in a 1-cup (250-g) measuring cup with chopsticks or a fork; fill cup with water to measure 1 cup (250 g). Pour flour into a medium bowl, add egg mixture, and blend lightly. Do not blend until smooth; it is okay to have lumps of flour.
- Test oil temperature: Drop a bit of batter in oil. If it sinks to the bottom, then comes up, the oil is not hot enough. If it sinks halfway, then comes up, the temperature is right.
- Make tempura: Begin with harder vegetables, such as broccoli. Using chopsticks, dip pieces into batter. Gently slide 5–6 pieces at a time into oil. Cook 3 minutes, turning, until golden brown. Drain on paper towels and then keep warm in low oven. Continue with all vegetables. If oil temperature goes down, add more oil and wait until it gets to right temperature. Skim off excess pieces of batter.
- Serve immediately, while vegetables are still crisp, with sauce.

Serves 4

8 mushrooms, rinsed and dried
1 medium green bell pepper, seeded, deveined, and cut into 2-inch (5-cm) pieces
1 small Japanese eggplant, sliced ¼ inch (6 mm) thick
8 broccoli florets

BATTER
1 large egg
ice-cold water
1 cup (150 g) sifted all-purpose flour
4 cups (1 L) vegetable oil suitable for deep-frying

DIPPING SAUCE
¼ cup (60 ml) tamari or soy sauce
1 teaspoon finely chopped fresh ginger

1 cup (250 g) red lentils

¼ cup (60 ml) vegetable oil

1 tablespoon mustard seeds

1 medium onion, peeled, halved, and chopped (about 1 cup)

½ teaspoon ground turmeric

4 cups (1 L) water

1 teaspoon sea salt

1 bay leaf

3 medium tomatoes, diced (about 1½ cups)

½ bunch fresh cilantro leaves, chopped (about ½ cup)

Red Lentil Dal for Rice

Bhutanese and Indian

Dzongsar Khyentse Rinpoche taught me this recipe one day in London, when I was preparing lunch for him. Lentils come in yellow, green, and red. The red ones cook the quickest, taking only twenty minutes. These split beans are rich in protein and are essential to the cuisine of India. They are always cooked first with turmeric, which helps with their digestibility. Seasonings are added at the end. In an Indian meal, dal is served with two other vegetable dishes, basmati rice (see page 180), chapatis (see page 166), and yogurt. The dal is more like a soup, and in an Indian home it is spooned over the rice, mashed together, and eaten with the fingers.

METHOD

Mind Refresher ❂ Prepare with the motivation to help and make others happy.

· Cover lentils with water, soak 10 minutes, and then rinse several times; set aside.
· Heat oil in a Chinese wok or large saucepan over medium-high heat. Add mustard seeds and cook 30 seconds or until seeds begin to turn color.
· Stir in onion, reduce heat to medium-low, and cook, uncovered, stirring occasionally, until onion begins to soften.
· Stir in drained lentils, add turmeric, and cook, uncovered, stirring occasionally, 3 minutes or until lentils begin to turn yellow.
· Add water, salt, and bay leaf, bring to a boil, reduce heat to low, cover, and cook 25 minutes or until lentils are almost dissolved and thickened.
· Stir in tomatoes and cilantro and cook 5 minutes to blend flavors.
· Serve with rice.

Serves 4–6

Chewy Brown Rice Meal in a Bowl

New Zealand

This simple dish is very filling and nutritious, and it uses the most delicious New Zealand seaweed. It is, however, an acquired taste—some adore it and others think it is the worst! Nutritional yeast, which offers complete protein and B vitamins, can be bought in natural foods stores. Chock-full of minerals, seaweeds (or sea vegetables) have been rediscovered in the past ten years. See page 193 for more information about nutritional yeast and seaweed. Lastly, tamari is a traditional Japanese soy sauce made from beans that have naturally fermented in wooden kegs for many months and are then pressed. Eat this meal when you want to get back into balance with no fuss.

1 cup (250 g) hot cooked brown rice

½ cup (125 g) hot cooked lentils, green or red

1 tablespoon nutritional yeast

1 teaspoon olive oil

2 teaspoons tamari

1 tablespoon karengo seaweed (a New Zealand seaweed), or dulse, nori, or wakame, soaked and chopped

⅛ teaspoon ground cayenne pepper

METHOD

· Mix rice, lentils, nutritional yeast, olive oil, tamari, seaweed, and cayenne in a bowl.
· Serve and eat in bowl.

Mind Refresher ✿ Appreciate your present-moment mind.

Serves 1

OTHER EASY RICE DISHES

Basmati rice: Mix cottage cheese, green onions, sea salt, and black pepper into cooked basmati rice. This combination is easy to digest and comforting to eat when the body has had too much rich food.

Herb rice: Mix brown rice with olive oil, lemon juice, and fresh seasonal herbs such as parsley, basil, or cilantro.

3 tablespoons vegetable oil

1 medium onion, peeled and diced (about 1 cup)

1 medium green bell pepper or celery, diced (about 1 cup)

8 ounces (250 g) fresh white mushrooms, thinly sliced (about 3 cups)

1 clove garlic peeled and finely chopped

1 cup (200 g) walnut pieces or slivered almonds

1 cup (200 g) brown rice, white rice, or a combination of grains

2½ cups (600 ml) vegetable broth

½ teaspoon sea salt

¼ teaspoon freshly ground black pepper

green onions, thinly sliced, or fresh flat-leaf parsley, chopped

Rich Walnut and Rice Casserole

North American

Americans love casseroles. They are convenient because they accommodate lots of different ingredient combinations and can cook while you are doing something else. This dish may be cooked in the oven or on the stove. It is generally served directly from the casserole pot with a salad or a tofu cutlet. Many cuisines include rice dishes like this. Flavored with cinnamon and cumin, it's Indian; cooked with coconut milk, it's Thai; prepared with tomato and corn, it's Spanish. Be creative—add what suits your mood.

METHOD

· Preheat oven to 350° F (180° C).

> **Mind Refresher** ✿ Stand straight, breathe normally, and concentrate on your breath; as the mind wanders, come back to your breath.

· Heat oil in a large skillet, over medium heat; stir in onions and cook, stirring occasionally, 10 minutes or until soft.

· Stir in green pepper, mushrooms, and garlic; cook, stirring occasionally, 3 minutes to release flavors.

· Add walnuts and rice; continue cooking 5 minutes, stirring occasionally.

· Pour into a medium casserole dish; stir in broth, salt, and pepper; cover and bake 1 hour or until liquid is absorbed.

· Garnish with green onions or parsley and serve from casserole.

Serves 4

VARIATIONS

Different grains: Instead of 1 cup rice, try using ½ cup (200 g) rice, ¼ cup (60 g) barley, and ¼ cup (60 g) bulgur or ¾ cup (75 g) brown rice with ¼ cup (60 g) wild rice.

Winter squash rice: Prepare as above with these ingredients: 1 medium onion, chopped; 2 cloves garlic, finely chopped; 1 sprig fresh rosemary; 1 tablespoon soy sauce; 1 cup (200 g) short-grain brown rice; 2 cups (500 g) yellow winter squash, cut into ½-inch (1.2-cm) pieces; salt and pepper; 2½ cups (600 ml) water. Serve topped with almonds and raisins.

Aromatic Herb Rice Stuffed in Green Peppers

Greek from Thessaloniki

Of eastern Mediterranean origins, *Thessaloniki gemista*, as this dish is called in Greece, comes from the verb "to fill up." Peppers are filled with rice that has been seasoned with fresh aromatic herbs, currants, and pine nuts. This dish was served for lunch every other day during summer at my friend's grandmother's house. She served it with a Greek salad, yogurt or feta cheese, bread, and a glass of retsina. Tomatoes may be used in place of the peppers.

METHOD

· Preheat oven to 350° F (180° C).
· Boil peppers and their tops in a large pot, 3 minutes; drain in a colander and set aside.
· Heat oil in a large skillet over medium heat; add onion and cook, stirring occasionally, until tender.

Mind Refresher ✿ Stir in ingredients with a present-moment mind.

· Stir in rice, herbs, tomatoes, nuts, currants, tomato paste, salt, and pepper; cook, stirring, 5 minutes.
· Add 1¼ cups (300 ml) water and bring to a boil; cook uncovered 10 minutes, stirring occasionally.
· Make sauce: Mix tomato sauce, ½ cup (125 ml) water, oil, and oregano in a small bowl.
· Pour sauce into an 8 x 8 x 2–inch (20 x 20 x 5–cm) baking dish and arrange peppers on top. To make peppers stand straight, slice off a little of the bottoms. Fill peppers three-quarters full with rice mixture. Drizzle with olive oil and top with pepper tops.
· Pour sauce around peppers.
· Cover dish tightly and bake 1 hour or until rice and peppers are cooked through.

Serves 4

4 medium green bell peppers, seeded and deveined, tops cut off but saved
3 tablespoons olive oil
1 medium onion, peeled and diced (about 1 cup)
¾ cup (160 g) long-grain rice
1½ cups (100 g) finely chopped fresh herbs: mint, dill or basil, and flat-leaf parsley
1 medium tomato, diced (about ½ cup)
⅓ cup (45 g) pine nuts or sunflower seeds
⅓ cup (60 g) currants or raisins
1 tablespoon tomato paste or ketchup
1 teaspoon sea salt
¼ teaspoon freshly ground black pepper
1¼ cups (300 ml) water
olive oil

SAUCE
1 can (8 ounces or 250 ml) plain tomato sauce
½ cup (125 ml) water
1 tablespoon olive oil
1 tablespoon finely chopped fresh oregano or 1 teaspoon dried oregano

3 tablespoons olive oil

1 medium onion, peeled, halved,
  and sliced (about 1 cup)

2 medium red bell peppers,
  seeded and cut into 1-inch
  (2.5-cm) pieces (about 2 cups)

3 medium tomatoes, peeled
  and roughly chopped (about
  1½ cups)

2 cloves garlic, peeled and finely
  chopped

2 bay leaves, crumbled

10 baby Yukon gold potatoes,
  halved (1 pound or 500 g)

2 medium carrots, peeled, halved
  lengthwise, and cut into ½-inch
  (1.2-cm) pieces (about 1½
  cups)

1¼ cup (310 ml) water (1 cup
  [250 ml] and ¼ cup [60 ml])

1 teaspoon sea salt

¼ teaspoon freshly ground black
  pepper

1 tablespoon cornstarch mixed
  with 1 tablespoon water

½ cup fresh cilantro leaves

SEITAN

10 ounces (300 g) seitan, cut into
  1-inch (2.5-cm) pieces

2 tablespoons vegetable oil

2 cloves garlic, peeled and finely
  chopped

2 tablespoons tamari

1 bay leaf, crumbled

Seitan Vegetable Stew

Portuguese, from Setubal

The charming coastal town of Setubal, south of Lisbon, has a beautiful port and lots of winding side streets. Tucked away on one of these streets' plazas is a restaurant called Bago de Arroz, offering simple, delicious, and nourishing vegetarian fare. The daily dishes always include brown rice or potatoes—the Portuguese love potatoes. This filling stew will satisfy nonvegetarians and vegetarians alike. Seitan (pronounced SAY-tan) is made from high wheat-gluten flour; it has a chewy texture and is a good meat substitute. It can be found in natural food stores or prepared from scratch (see page 190). Enjoy this Portuguese stew with a salad and bread.

METHOD

> **Mind Refresher** ✿ **Make the dish with the motivation
> of benefiting others.**

· Heat oil in casserole pot over medium heat. Stir in onion and cook,
  stirring occasionally, until soft.
· Add red pepper, tomato, garlic, and bay leaves; cook, uncovered,
  3–5 minutes, stirring occasionally.
· Stir in potatoes, carrots, 1 cup (250 ml) water, salt, and pepper. Bring
  to a boil.
· Reduce heat to low, cover, and cook 20 minutes or until carrots and
  potatoes are tender.
· Prepare seitan while stew is cooking: Heat oil in a medium skillet
  over medium heat. Stir in seitan, garlic, tamari, and bay leaf.
  Cook, stirring, about 2 minutes or until seitan is well seasoned and
  begins to brown. Stir in ¼ cup (60 ml) water to deglaze the pan.
  Cook 1 minute more in juice. Set aside.
· When carrots and potatoes are tender, add seitan to stew. Continue
  cooking 5 minutes to blend flavors.
· Mix in cornstarch paste and cook a few minutes more. Stew can be
  made ahead to this point.
· Just before serving, stir in cilantro leaves.

Serves 4

Light Couscous with Seven Vegetables

Moroccan

Seven is an auspicious number in Moroccan culture, as it is in many cultures. This multi-vegetable stew is served over hot, raisin-studded couscous, with a spicy tomato sauce on the side. It makes a nice presentation dish for company as well as an easy stew for the family. The vegetables can be changed to suit your tastes and whatever you have on hand. Couscous is precooked, coarsely ground semolina (durum wheat with the bran and germ removed); a light, quickly cooked grain, it is frequently used in North African cuisine. Sip mint tea with this dish, and enjoy the experience as if you were a guest in a Moroccan household; you feel like a king or queen with their service and hospitality.

METHOD

- Heat oil in a soup pot over medium-high heat; stir in onions and cook, stirring occasionally, 5 minutes or until soft.
- Stir in carrots and turnips, reduce heat to medium-low, cover, and cook 10 minutes.
- Stir in remaining ingredients, except zucchini and harissa, cover, and cook 40 minutes.
- Stir in zucchini, cover, and cook 20 minutes or until vegetables are cooked through.
- Make couscous: Put chickpeas in a small bowl and cover with some of the hot vegetable broth. Put raisins in another small bowl and cover with hot water. Place couscous in a medium bowl and stir in oil. Pour boiling water onto couscous, cover with a towel, and let stand 10 minutes. Fluff with a fork. Drain chickpeas and raisins; stir into couscous.
- Drain broth from vegetables into a bowl; mix with harissa to desired spice level and set aside to use as sauce for couscous.
- Serve couscous on a platter in a mound topped with vegetables. Pass sauce on the side.

> **Mind Refresher** ❁ Serve with loving kindness.

Serves 6

TRADITIONAL METHOD FOR COOKING COUSCOUS

Put couscous into a fine strainer in the sink. Pour boiling water over couscous. Salt to taste. Add a little olive oil and rub couscous between your hands to incorporate. Set the strainer above a bowl of hot water and cover with a towel. Let sit 5 minutes. Repeat this procedure three times from the beginning. Fluff couscous with a fork before serving.

3 tablespoons olive oil

2 medium onions, peeled, halved, and sliced (about 3 cups)

3 medium carrots, peeled and cut into ½-inch (1.2-cm) diagonal slices (about 3 cups)

2 medium turnips, peeled and cut into 1½-inch (3.7-cm) pieces (about 4 cups)

1 medium eggplant, peeled and cut into 1½-inch (3.7-cm) pieces (about 4 cups)

2 green bell peppers, seeded, veins removed, and cut into 1½-inch (3.7-cm) pieces (about 4 cups)

3 medium zucchini, peeled and cut into 2-inch (5-cm) pieces (about 3 cups)

1 can (14 ounces or 400 g) peeled and diced tomatoes with juice

2 cloves garlic, finely chopped

3 cups (720 ml) vegetable broth

1 tablespoon tomato paste or ketchup

1½ teaspoons ground coriander

1 teaspoon ground ginger

½ teaspoon ground nutmeg

½ teaspoon ground paprika

¼ teaspoon ground turmeric

¼ teaspoon ground cayenne

2 teaspoons sea salt

harissa or chili paste

COUSCOUS

1 can (15 ounces) (450 g) chickpeas, drained and rinsed

½ cup (90 g) golden raisins, soaked

3 cups (625 g) couscous

2 tablespoon olive oil

3 cups (720 ml) boiling water

Creamy Polenta with Mushroom Sauce

Italian, from the Abruzzi region

The traditional Abruzzi way to serve coarse ground polenta is *sulla tavola*, on a board. The polenta is cooked to a creamy consistency, poured on a board at the center of the table, and then topped with tomato sauce and finished with freshly grated Parmigiano cheese. Everyone digs in and eats until no more is left. Traditionally polenta is cooked in an unlined copper pot called a *paiolo*, found in every family home. When you want to prepare this dish quickly, use fine cornmeal; it takes 5 to 10 minutes to cook. It goes well with the Olive Oil and Mint Orange Salad (page 50), baked eggplant drizzled with olive oil and oregano, and Chianti.

METHOD

- Bring water and salt to a boil in a large pot over high heat.
- Slowly add polenta in a steady stream, stirring continuously with a long wooden spoon.

> **Mind Refresher** ✿ **Stand straight, breathe normally, and reflect on patience while stirring the polenta.**

- Lower heat to a gentle boil and continue stirring 30 minutes or until polenta pulls away from the sides and is not gritty. You may need to use more water as it cooks. Use boiling water.
- Cover pot with buttered waxed paper and place in a warm-water bath. Polenta stays hot up to 3 hours.
- Make sauce: Heat oil in a large skillet over medium-high heat; add onion and cook, stirring occasionally, 10 minutes or until onion begins to carmelize; stir in tomatoes, garlic, and mushrooms, reduce heat to medium-low, and cook, uncovered, 15 minutes; stir in basil, salt, and pepper.
- Pour hot polenta onto a clean, unfinished wooden table or a large chopping board, 18 x 18 inches (45 cm x 45 cm), and shape into a thick circle.
- Make a 4-inch (10-cm) indent in the center, pour in tomato sauce, and sprinkle with cheese.

Serves 6

8 cups (2 L) water
1 tablespoon sea salt
2 cups (325 g) medium-coarse polenta

SAUCE
4 tablespoons olive oil
1 medium onion, peeled, halved, and sliced (about 1½ cup)
3 (14-ounce or 400-g) cans diced tomatoes (42 ounces or 1,200 g)
2 cloves garlic, peeled and halved
½ ounce (15 g) dried mushrooms, soaked in hot water and finely chopped (about ¼ cup)
½ bunch chopped fresh basil leaves (about ½ cup)
sea salt and freshly ground black pepper
freshly grated Parmigiano or Romano cheese

VARIATIONS
- Let cool and then slice into pieces for frying.
- Mix in diced mozzarella or fontina cheese.
- Use half water and half milk to make dish more flavorful.
- Cut into slices, put overlapping in buttered baking pan, drizzle with olive oil, and top with lots of grated Parmiggiano cheese. Bake at 400° F (200° C) until browned.

3 cups (325 g) (packed) fresh
 whole-wheat breadcrumbs
1 cup (200 g) (packed) ground
 walnuts
1 cup (125 g) finely chopped
 walnuts
½ cup (60 g) nutritional yeast
2 tablespoons tamari
½ cup (125 ml) tomato juice
4 tablespoons (60 g) butter
2½ large onions (1 pound or
 500 g), diced
3–4 large cloves garlic, finely
 chopped
2 large eggs, beaten
1 cup (140 g) (packed) shredded
 cheddar cheese
½ teaspoon sea salt
½ teaspoon freshly ground black
 pepper
1 bunch fresh flat-leaf parsley,
 finely chopped (about 1 cup)
½ cup (60 g) shredded cheddar
 cheese

Walnut Cheddar Loaf

New Zealand, from Christ Church

This recipe comes from a vegetarian family in New Zealand who always struggled to come up with something great to serve for Christmas dinner. They found the answer to their struggles with this recipe. The walnuts and breadcrumbs impart a very hearty, meaty flavor, making this a perfect holiday dish. Serve it with gravy, mashed potatoes, peas, roasted pumpkin, carrots, and parsnips. In New Zealand, a meal is always meat plus three veggies; replace the meat with this dish at any time of year and be completely satisfied.

METHOD

- Preheat oven to 350° F (180° C) and lightly grease a 9 x 5 x 3–inch (23 x 13 x 6–cm) loaf pan.
- Combine breadcrumbs, walnuts, nutritional yeast, tamari, and tomato juice in a large mixing bowl; set aside.

> **Mind Refresher** ✿ **Stand straight, breathe normally, and watch your in-and-out breath for 30 seconds.**

- Melt butter in a medium skillet over medium heat. Add onions and garlic, cook, and stir frequently until translucent. Add to breadcrumb mixture.
- Mix eggs, grated cheese, salt, pepper, and parsley with breadcrumb mixture.
- Pack mixture into loaf pan and bake, uncovered, 1 hour.
- Cover loaf with shredded cheese and bake 10 minutes or until cheese is bubbly.
- Serve sliced with gravy and love.

Serves 6

FRESH BREADCRUMBS

To make fresh breadcrumbs, tear bread into small pieces and lay on a baking sheet. Bake at 400° F (200° C) 10 minutes or until brown and hard. Cool. Put in a plastic sack and break up with a rolling pin or food processor.

Feta-Topped Garden Vegetable Pasta

Australian

This dish is easy to serve because it is simply tossed together in a serving bowl and garnished with feta and parsley. The feta, a crumbly goat cheese found in Greek and Middle Eastern cooking, is added at the end to pick up the flavors with its saltiness. Fresh Italian flat-leaf parsley has more flavor than the curly leaf kind. It can be found in markets, but it is easy to grow in your garden. Fusilli pasta looks like corkscrews and has a chewy texture that works well for tossed pasta dishes. Note that such dishes are much more interesting when you cut the vegetables into different shapes. Any leftovers can be served the next day as a salad with balsamic vinegar, olive oil, and olives.

METHOD

> **Mind Refresher** ✿ Stand straight, breathe normally, and concentrate on your breath for 30 seconds. Cut vegetables with a knife of awareness.

- Heat 1 tablespoon oil in a medium skillet over medium-high heat. Stir in mushrooms and cook, stirring occasionally, until all water evaporates. Remove mushrooms from skillet and set aside.
- Heat 2 tablespoons oil in skillet over medium heat. Stir in onion, cover, and cook, stirring occasionally, 10 minutes or until slightly brown.
- Stir in tomatoes, zucchini, and carrots, cover, and cook 8–10 minutes or until vegetables are to desired doneness.
- Stir in mushrooms, salt, and pepper.
- Toss vegetables and pasta in a serving bowl.
- Sprinkle feta and parsley around edges of bowl, finishing with freshly ground black pepper.

Serves 4

1 pound (500 g) curly fusilli pasta, cooked according to package directions

4 ounces (125 g) mushrooms, thinly sliced (about 1½ cups)

3 tablespoons olive oil, divided

1 medium onion, peeled, halved, and sliced (about 1 cup)

1 can (15 ounces or 450 g) diced tomatoes or 4 medium tomatoes, peeled and diced

1 medium zucchini, halved and sliced (about 1½ cups)

1 medium carrot, peeled and cut in thin, matchlike sticks (about 1 cup)

sea salt and freshly ground black pepper

½ cup (60 g) feta cheese

generous handful finely chopped fresh flat-leaf parsley (about ⅓ cup)

4 cups (250 g) cooked pasta (if
    spaghetti, cut up)
2 cups (350 g) cooked vegetables
    (broccoli, zucchini, carrots, bell
    peppers, mushrooms, peas)
1 cup (150 g) fresh breadcrumbs,
    grated cheese, or a mixture
    of both
2 tablespoons (30 g) butter, cut
    into small cubes

WHITE SAUCE

4 tablespoons (60 g) butter
¼ cup (35 g) all-purpose flour
3 cups (720 ml) whole milk
2 cloves garlic, peeled and finely
    chopped
⅛ teaspoon ground nutmeg
1 teaspoon sea salt
¼ teaspoon freshly ground black
    pepper

Vegetable Gratin with Leftover Pasta

French

Gratin means "crusted." A number of ingredients can make the crust for a gratin—this recipe calls for cheese and breadcrumbs. The dish offers a good way to use leftover pasta or to feed a lot of people. Using leftovers lends originality to your cooking. An old French chef named Josephine would say, "I always take everything out of my refrigerator to see what I have, and then I decide what to make for the day. That way I don't waste anything." This recipe is straightforward and plain; herbs, garlic, and onions can be added for more flavor. Be creative!

METHOD

· Preheat oven to 425° F (220° C).
· Butter a 13 x 9 x 2–inch (33 x 23 x 5–cm) baking dish.
· Mix pasta and vegetables in baking dish.
· Make white sauce: Melt butter in a medium saucepan over low heat, stir in flour, and cook, stirring,1 minute. Using wire whisk, slowly whisk milk into butter and flour paste until smooth. Season with garlic, nutmeg, salt, and pepper and cook, covered, 15 minutes or until sauce begins to thicken.

> **Mind Refresher** ✿ **Stand straight, breath normally,
> and concentrate on the in-and-out breath as you pour
> the sauce over the pasta.**

· Pour sauce over pasta.
· Sprinkle with breadcrumbs and cheese and dot with butter.
· Bake 45 minutes or until crusty brown.

Serves 4–6

FRESH BREADCRUMBS

To make fresh breadcrumbs, grate leftover bread (French bread works well) with a grater or a food processor to create rough and irregular pieces.

No-Cook Sauce with Pasta

Italian

This is the simplest way to make pasta: one pot to boil the water and one bowl to mix the sauce and serve the pasta. Pasta comes in many varieties, including whole-wheat and refined white flour. Both of these are made from durum wheat, but the white is striped of its bran and wheat germ. Whole-wheat pasta has a rich, nutty flavor because no fiber has been removed. Try them both. For those allergic to wheat, there is also pasta made from brown or white rice or from whole corn. The Japanese have pastas called soba, made from buckwheat, and udon, made from whole-wheat flour. Different pastas create different flavors, so experiment.

1 pound (500 g) pasta
¼ cup (60 ml) olive oil
4 medium tomatoes, diced (about 2 cups)
¼ cup (60 ml) crumbled goat or feta cheese or grated Parmesan cheese
¼ cup (60 ml) olives, pitted and chopped
2 cloves garlic, peeled and finely chopped
handful finely chopped fresh basil, parsley, or other herbs (about 2 tablespoons)
sea salt and freshly ground black pepper

METHOD

· Cook pasta according to package directions.
· Mix oil, tomatoes, cheese, olives, garlic, and herbs in a medium serving bowl.
· Drain pasta and toss with sauce.

> **Mind Refresher** ✿ Stand straight and relax into tasting the pasta.

· Season to taste with salt and pepper.
· Serve immediately.

Serves 4

SAUCE VARIATIONS

Avocado chili sauce: Follow the above recipe but replace cheese and olives with 1 small green chili, finely chopped, and 1 avocado, diced; for the herbs, use fresh cilantro leaves.

Pesto sauce: See recipe on page 132 for this classic pasta sauce.

1 tablespoon butter

1 tablespoon olive oil

1 pound (500 g) fresh white mushrooms, rinsed and thinly sliced

2 cloves garlic, peeled and finely chopped

1 bunch finely chopped fresh flat-leaf parsley (about 1 cup)

½ cup (125 g) crème fraîche or 1 tablespoon flour mixed with ½ cup (125 ml) heavy cream

sea salt and freshly ground black pepper

PASTRY

1 cup (150 g) all-purpose flour

pinch sea salt

6 tablespoons (90 g) cold salted butter, cut into ½-inch (1.2-cm) cubes

2–3 tablespoons ice-cold water

HERBES DE PROVENCE

The mixture varies according to availability of the herbs.

Thyme, 1 teaspoon

Summer savory, 1 teaspoon

Lavender, ½ teaspoon

Rosemary, ¼ teaspoon

Fennel, ¼ teaspoon

Oregano, ½ teaspoon

Sage, ¼ teaspoon

Basil (optional), ¼ teaspoon

Garlic Mushroom Tart

French, from Midi-Pyrenees

The French grandmother of a friend of mine always served this dish to her family for Sunday lunch, alongside roast beef. The version described here leaves the roast behind. Instead, serve it with a soup or a salad to make a satisfying meal. In the fall, use wild mushrooms and fresh herbs, such as thyme, fennel, sage, or winter savory. The thin and light crust accents the full flavor of the mushrooms. The secret to the crust is to butter the tart pan.

METHOD

· Preheat oven to 425° F (220° C).

· Lightly butter a 9-inch (22.5-cm) French tart pan or an 8-inch (20-cm) pie pan.

· Make pastry: Stir flour and salt in a mixing bowl or food processor. Rub butter into flour between your fingertips, or process quickly, until mixture is like cornmeal. Mix in water quickly with your hand to form a ball. Cover and let rest in the refrigerator 15–30 minutes, while preparing mushrooms.

Mind Refresher ✿ Appreciate whatever is happening.

· Heat oil in a medium skillet over medium-high heat; stir in mushrooms and cook, stirring, until mushrooms are cooked and there is no more liquid.

· Add garlic, salt, and pepper, and set aside.

· Mix parsley and crème fraîche in a small bowl.

· Flatten pastry into a 1-inch (2.5-cm) circle on a lightly floured board. Roll out pastry from the center in all directions, to the size of tart pan. Fold pastry in half to move it to the pan; place pastry in pan, unfold, and press onto sides.

· Pour mushrooms into tart shell and spread parsley sauce on top.

· Bake on lower shelf of oven 35–40 minutes or until crust is brown and firm to touch.

· Let sit 10 minutes before serving.

Serves 4

Pizza-Style Cheese Crisp

North American, from Arizona

Similar to a pizza but crisp and made with a flour tortilla similar to a chapati, this is a quick meal for kids. Many of Arizona's Mexican restaurants bring a huge one of these to the center of the table as an appetizer. Typical varieties are plain cheese, cheese with chili strips, or cheese with avocado slices, all served with fresh tomato salsa (see page 119) on the side. Innovations include goat cheese with red pepper sauce and basil; sun-dried tomatoes, goat cheese, and roasted garlic; and provolone cheese, olives, red peppers, and basil. Let your imagination go wild.

1 flour tortilla (8–10 inches or 20–25 cm)

vegetable oil

½ cup (60 g) shredded longhorn, Monterey Jack, or other melting cheese

METHOD

· Preheat oven to 400° F (200° C).
· Brush flour tortilla very lightly with oil.
· Place on ungreased cookie sheet.
· Bake tortilla until it begins to crisp; watch closely.
· Sprinkle with cheese and other toppings. Return to oven and bake until cheese melts.
· Slice in quarters and serve with tomato salsa.

Mind Refresher ❂ Serve with a kind heart.

Serves 1–2

2 cups (300 g) buckwheat flour
½ teaspoon sea salt
3 cups (720 ml) tepid water
vegetable oil
apple slice
2 large eggs (optional)

Nutty Buckwheat Galettes

French, from Brittany

Galettes and crêpes are a culinary staple for the people of Brittany, where they are found in restaurants and at all the markets. The main difference between galettes and crêpes is the composition of the batter: Galettes are made with buckwheat flour (*sarrasin,* in Breton), crêpes with wheat flour. Also, galettes are savory, while crêpes are generally sweet. The traditional way of making galettes is to mix the batter energetically with your hand and cook it on a cast-iron cooking slab (*bilig,* in Breton). They are then filled with savory ingredients, folded to make a square or triangle, and eaten with a fork and knife, accompanied by a glass of apple cider or farm-fresh buttermilk (*lait ribot*). Every household has its particular recipe; this one is much easier than most and uses a nonstick skillet. Galettes are especially hardy and satisfying served alongside an escarole salad with a strong vinaigrette.

METHOD

- Put flour and salt in a medium mixing bowl. Whisk water slowly into flour until the consistency is that of cream.

> **Mind Refresher** ✿ **Stand straight, breathe normally, and keep your focus on the breath while whisking batter.**

- Whisk batter energetically until air bubbles appear on surface.
- Cover and let sit 1–3 hours at room temperature or overnight in the refrigerator.
- Whisk again, adding a little water if too thick.
- Heat a 9-inch (22.5-cm) nonstick skillet over medium-high heat until almost smoking.
- Brush with oil using an apple slice and reduce heat to medium.
- Ladle batter (about ¼ cup or 60 g) into pan, swirling it to spread evenly. Batter should be thin; pour back any excess. If batter does not spread, whisk 2 eggs into batter bowl.
- Cook 2 minutes or until brown. Flip over with a fork to cook other side.
- Transfer to a plate and make remaining galettes, stacking them on top of each other.

- Return 1 cooked galette to the pan, place filling in the middle, and fold 4 sides toward center to make a square, leaving some filling exposed. Heat until filling is cooked and brush with butter.
- Serve immediately, seam up or down.

Makes 12

FILLING SUGGESTIONS

Savory galette fillings include cheese, eggs, sautéed mushrooms and herb cream, tomatoes and garlic, ratatouille, steamed broccoli and garlic béchamel sauce, and warm spinach and goat cheese. To make an egg-filled galette, try the following: Break egg on center of galette; use a fork to break up white around yolk; sprinkle with cheese and fold 4 sides of galette toward yolk, leaving soft-cooked yolk showing.

4 cups (250 g) finely chopped
   fresh herbs (dill, chives,
   flat-leafed parsley, and cilantro)
4–6 green lettuce leaves, finely
   chopped (about 2 cups)
2 green onions, thinly sliced
6 eggs, beaten
sea salt and freshly ground pepper
4 tablespoons olive oil
   (2 tablespoons and
   2 tablespoons)

CUCUMBER SAUCE
1 medium English cucumber,
   peeled, seeded, and diced
   (about 1½ cups)
½ cup (125 g) plain yogurt
2 tablespoons fromage blanc,
   Greek-style yogurt, or sour
   cream
3 tablespoons golden raisins,
   soaked and drained
2 sprigs fresh mint, stalks
   removed and leaves finely
   chopped

Baked Eggs with Fresh Herbs
Persian, from Rasht

Rasht is an Iranian village near the Caspian Sea with a humid climate favorable to growing fresh vegetables and herbs. This dish is called *kookoo sabzi*, which means "green eggs." Feel free to experiment, using anything green. The secret is to avoid overcooking the eggs. This classic dish is served in people's homes and used for picnics in spring, when there are many fresh herbs. In winter it is made with finely grated carrots, onions, and potatoes. It is served with a cucumber, raisin, and mint yogurt sauce and a flat bread called *sangak*.

METHOD

· Preheat oven to 425° F (220° C).
· Make sauce: Mix cucumber, yogurt, fromage blanc, raisins, and mint in a small bowl. Set aside.

Mind Refresher ✿ Appreciate the aroma of the herbs.

· Heat 2 tablespoons oil in a 9-inch (22.5-cm) ovenproof skillet. Add herbs, lettuce, and onions. Stir occasionally and cook 5 minutes to soften. Transfer to plate to cool.
· Mix herbs and eggs in a medium bowl. Season with salt and pepper.
· Heat 2 tablespoons oil in skillet over medium heat. Pour egg mixture into hot oil, reduce heat to medium-low, and cook, undisturbed, for 2 minutes or until bottom is firm and brown.
· Transfer skillet to oven. Bake about 5 minutes, just until top is firm.
· Cut into wedges and serve with cucumber sauce. Invert cooked eggs onto a plate to display the browned side when served.

Serves 4

5 large eggs, separated

½ cup (125 g) finely chopped or shredded vegetables

¼ cup (30 g) shredded cheese (optional)

¼ cup (30 g) chopped, fresh flat-leaf parsley

2 green onions, thinly sliced or finely chopped

1 teaspoon sea salt

¼ teaspoon freshly ground black pepper

2 tablespoons vegetable oil

Pan Soufflé Eggs

Brazilian

This egg dish is a staple in one Brazilian couple's Rio de Janeiro kitchen. She kept some vegetables and eggs in the kitchen at all times, so there was always something to eat. The key to this dish is that the egg whites are folded in, resulting in a light texture. Along with cheese and fresh herbs, any vegetables can be added to the eggs—green pepper, grated carrot, zucchini, broccoli. Check out your fridge and see what is on hand. The dish is served for lunch with rice and salad, for dinner with rice and black beans, and as a sandwich between bread. Try also serving it with a condiment—Red Tomato-Chili Salsa (see page 119) or Spicy Soy-Sauced Tomatoes (see page 121).

METHOD

> **Mind Refresher** ✿ Stand straight. Beat out your mind's poisons as you beat eggs.

- With a fork or hand mixer, beat egg whites with a pinch of salt in a bowl until they are stiff and hold a peak.
- Beat yolks in another bowl until smooth.
- Add yolks to egg whites and beat a few seconds, until mixed.
- Gently fold in vegetables, cheese, parsley, green onions, salt, and pepper.
- Heat oil in a 10-inch (25-cm) nonstick skillet over medium heat. Pour in egg mixture and cook until it begins to firm around edges and underside is brown.
- Turn eggs over by placing a plate the size of skillet on top and inverting eggs onto it. Slip eggs back into skillet to finish cooking and browning.
- Transfer to a serving plate and cut into wedges.

Serves 2–4

Crisp Tortilla Topped with Egg and Salsa

Mexican

Corn tortillas are a staple of Mexican cuisine. Made from a special corn flour that is pressed and fried in a skillet, they are readily available in most grocery stores and Mexican markets. This dish, commonly known as *huevos rancheros,* makes a delicious lunch or dinner for the family, served with refried pinto beans (found canned in stores) and a salad of shredded cabbage with guacamole (see page 129).

2 tablespoons vegetable oil, divided
1 corn tortilla
1 large egg
2 tablespoons tomato salsa (see page 119)
1 tablespoon shredded cheddar or Monterey Jack cheese, or crumbled feta

METHOD

· Preheat broiler.
· Heat 1 tablespoon oil in a nonstick skillet over medium-high heat; fry tortilla until crisp and drain on a paper towel. Transfer crisp tortilla to a baking sheet.
· Heat 1 tablespoon oil in a skillet over medium heat; fry egg until white is firm but yolk is still soft.
· Place on tortilla.
· Spoon tomato salsa (see page 119) over egg and top with grated cheese. Put under broiler for a few seconds to melt cheese.
· Transfer to a serving plate.

Mind Refresher ❂ Serve with loving kindness.

Serves 1

BEANS

To cook beans: Rinse 1 pound (500 g) dried beans (black, pink or pinto, adzuki), making sure there are no stones. Put beans into a pot and cover with 12 cups (3 L) water. Add ½ onion, roughly sliced, and 2 tablespoons oil. Bring to a boil, reduce heat, and simmer, covered, 1–2 hours, or until beans are almost tender. Add 1 tablespoon salt and cook 30 minutes more. When finished, the beans should be completely soft and the broth thick.

To make refried beans: Heat ¼ cup (60 ml) oil in a skillet and cook ½ onion, chopped, until soft. Add 1 cup (250 g) beans with their broth and mash well as they cook over very high flame. Gradually add the remaining beans, little by little, mashing them. When the puree begins to dry out and sizzle at the edges, it is ready.

Bull's-Eye Eggs

North American, from Seattle

A friend's father used to make this dish as a weekend treat when she was a child. Kids like the trick of the egg inside the bread. Using good-quality eggs and flavorful whole-wheat bread makes it delicious. The French eat their eggs for lunch or dinner, and this dish can work as a meal at any time of day.

2 slices whole-wheat bread

4 tablespoons (60 g) softened butter

2 large eggs

METHOD

· Using a small glass, cut 2½-inch (6.2-cm) circular holes in bread slices.

> **Mind Refresher ✿** Stand straight and keep your attention on the knife as you spread the butter.

· Spread most of butter on both sides of slices, making sure to reach all corners.
· Place slices in a nonstick skillet and cook over medium-low heat until browned.
· Turn slices over and put remaining butter in holes.
· Crack an egg into each hole. Cook, covered, until white is cooked through and yolk is soft, or until egg is cooked to your preference.
· Transfer to a plate and serve.

Serves 1

Offering Prayers

It is a custom in many cultures to offer food while thinking of our connection to all beings, in order to develop less attachment to our food and our bodies and to appreciate the good causes and conditions allowing us to have food. These are the prayers I say before each meal.

May this food nourish my body, speech, and mind,
so I may nourish and serve the body, speech, and mind of others.
I offer this food to all beings, may they never go hungry.

A TRADITIONAL TIBETAN BUDDHIST PRAYER

ༀ། །སྟོན་པ་བླ་མེད་སངས་རྒྱས་རིན་པོ་ཆེ། །སྐྱོབ་པ་བླ་མེད་དམ་ཆོས་རིན་པོ་ཆེ། །འཛིན་པ་བླ་མེད་དགེ་འདུན་རིན་པོ་ཆེ། །སྐྱབས་གནས་དཀོན་མཆོག་གསུམ་ལ་མཆོད་པ་འབུལ།། །།

ༀ། །སྟོན་པ་བླ་མེད་སངས་རྒྱས་རིན་པོ་ཆེ། །
སྐྱོབ་པ་བླ་མེད་དམ་ཆོས་རིན་པོ་ཆེ། །
འཛིན་པ་བླ་མེད་དགེ་འདུན་རིན་པོ་ཆེ། །
སྐྱབས་གནས་དཀོན་མཆོག་གསུམ་ལ་མཆོད་པ་འབུལ།། །།

Tönpa lamé sangyé rinpoché
To the precious Buddha, teacher unsurpassed

Kyob-pa lamé tamchö rinpoché
To the precious Dharma, unsurpassed protection

Drenpa lamé gendun rinpoché
To the precious Sangha, unsurpassed guides

Kyabné könchok sum la chöpar bul.
To the triple place of refuge I offer this nourishment.

Compassion

As a follower of the Buddha's teachings, I consider that a human life is one of the most precious vehicles for those wishing to achieve freedom once and forever, for oneself and for others.

Thus the food we eat is as important as the medicine that we take to overcome illness: It is the means to maintain this vehicle in good condition. I believe that it is essential to our physical and mental health and well-being to choose foods that are organically grown, free from pesticides and harmful chemicals, and more particularly foods that don't involve, from production to consumption, physical or mental suffering of either animals or humans.

One of Buddha's most crucial messages is this: the view is interdependence; the practice is nonviolence, love, and compassion.

A large proportion of the numerous incurable and manmade diseases in the world of today stem from these two causes: poisonous chemicals and the torments of the animals destined for the food industry. What do we expect? I humbly request those who wish for a healthy, happy life, free from mental and physical problems, to reflect on this. I wish for the health and peace of many human beings, while saving many, many animals from suffering.

—PEMA WANGYAL RINPOCHE
La Sonnerie,
Dordogne, France

CHAPTER 5

Side Dishes

for Extra Courage

Eating Everything and Never Satisfied

Sarvabhaksha, the one who eats everything, lived in the kingdom of King Singhachandra, who ruled the city of Abhira. He was born in a low caste. His stomach was so large that he ate all that he saw in front of him. One day he couldn't find anything to eat and was resting in a corner. His thinking was occupied by the desire for food.

The glorious Guru Saraha came along and asked him, "Why are you here?"

Sarvabhaksha replied, "The fire in my stomach is so big. Nothing that I eat satisfies me. Today I suffer because I have nothing to eat."

Guru Saraha replied, "If you aren't able to endure hunger for even one day, what will it be like when you are reborn as a *preta* [hungry ghost]? Their suffering is because of their actions of greed."

"Where does one find these beings?" asked Sarvabhaska.

"Look at them!" said Saraha, pointing everywhere.

After Saraha explained it to him, Sarvabhaska asked how one truly escaped this fate. Saraha then initiated him in the way of the Bodhisattva (Bodhicaryavatara) and instructed him as follows:

Meditate that your stomach is as empty as the sky.
Your digestion is like the fire at the end of time.
The entire visible world is your nourishment and your drink.
And let it disappear as you devour it.

Sarvabhaska meditated with such devotion that the sun and the moon became afraid and hid in the interior of the mountain of Meru. Everyone cried out, "The light is going out!" The *dakinis* (celestial messengers) invoked the grand Brahma, who came down to Sarvabhaska and told him, "At present you have devoured all the things; now meditate without them." The sun and the moon reappeared, and the entire world rejoiced.

After following this instruction for the next fifteen years, Sarvabhaska realized the union of all things and emptiness, achieving *siddhi* accomplishments (enlightenment). For six hundred years thereafter, he worked for the happiness of others. Then he left to the celestial realm, accompanied by a million disciples.

— **JIGME KHYENTSE RINPOCHE,** *Tibetan*

6–8 (60 g) fresh or dried chilis
(Anaheim, jalapeño, or
serrano), seeded to minimize
hotness, if desired

½ cup (125 ml) water

1½ cups (200 g) shredded melting
cheese, such as Cantal,
Monterey Jack, or fontina

2 tablespoons (30 g) butter

3 cloves garlic, peeled and finely
chopped (optional)

½ teaspoon sea salt

¼ cup thinly sliced green onions
(optional)

Chili and Cheese Paste for Rice
Bhutanese

In Bhutan this dish is called *emma datsi* (*emma* means "chili" and *datsi* means "cheese paste"). Bhutan has two types of dried chiles: red ones, which are fully ripened green chiles that have been dried in the sun, and white ones, which are picked green, boiled, and then dried in the sun. How much chile you use depends on your tolerance level. The Bhutanese can tolerate a lot of chilies—the hotter the better. The monks love to eat this dish over rice.

METHOD

> **Mind Refresher ✿** Create the intention for the
> right causes and conditions. When we are rushed,
> distracted, or in a bad mood,
> the food we prepare never tastes very good.

- Cut chilies in lengthwise strips.
- Place water and chilies in a medium saucepan over high heat and bring to a boil. Reduce heat to low and cook, covered, 5 minutes or until chiles are soft.
- Stir in cheese, butter, garlic, and salt. Cook, covered, 2 minutes more.
- Remove from heat, stir in green onions, cover, and let sit a few minutes, until mixture develops a paste consistency.
- Serve over rice.

Serves 2–4

Quick Mushrooms and Cheese for Rice

Bhutanese

Many varieties of mushrooms can be found in the countryside of
Bhutan, which is nestled in the Himalayas and bordered by Tibet,
Sikkim, and Bangladesh. This dish combines mushrooms and cheese,
usually a yak-milk cheese in Bhutan. *Shamu datsi,* as this dish is called,
is served with rice and makes a nice side vegetable dish with *emma datsi*
(see previous recipe).

METHOD

· Place mushrooms, water, butter, and salt in a medium saucepan over
high heat and bring to a boil. Reduce heat to medium-low, cover,
and cook 5 minutes.
· Stir in cheese, tomato, and green onion, cover, and cook 2 minutes or
until cheese melts.
· Pour into a serving dish and serve with rice.

Mind Refresher ✿ Appreciate whatever is happening.

Serves 2–4

8 ounces (250 g) thinly sliced
fresh mushrooms (about
3 cups)
½ cup (125 ml) water
2 tablespoons (30 g) butter
½ teaspoon sea salt
1 cup (100 g) shredded melting
cheese, such as Cantal,
Monterey Jack, or fontina
1 medium tomato, diced (about
½ cup)
2 green onions, thinly sliced
(about ½ cup)

4 tablespoons vegetable oil,
  divided
1 pound (500 g) long beans or
  green beans, tips removed,
  cut into 2-inch (5-cm) pieces
1 tablespoon water
1 tablespoon finely chopped garlic
1 tablespoon finely chopped
  shallots
1 tablespoon thinly sliced green
  onions
1 teaspoon finely chopped fresh
  ginger root
1 teaspoon chopped fresh small
  green or red chili
2 tablespoons preserved
  vegetables (optional)

SEASONING
1 tablespoon light soy sauce
1 tablespoon dark soy sauce
2 teaspoons cornstarch
1 teaspoon toasted sesame
  seed oil
¼ teaspoon ground black pepper
pinch sugar

Garlicky Treasured Beans
Chinese, from Szechwan

Long beans generally are very popular in Southeast Asia, and this dish is a particular favorite. Preserved vegetables, found in Asian markets, are usually made with daikon or turnips and have a very salty flavor. Chinese cooks use both light and dark soy sauces; the dark is not salty but has a heavy taste and gives color, while the light is saltier but does not have much color. Just use a common soy sauce as a substitute for both. Sugar is used with salt in Chinese cooking because the combination brings out the flavor of both without having to use much of either. Try this method to cook leafy greens.

METHOD

· Heat 2 tablespoons oil in a wok or skillet over high heat; add beans and cook, stirring, a few minutes.
· Add water, reduce heat to medium-low, cover, and cook, stirring occasionally, 5 minutes or until tender. Remove beans from wok and set aside.
· Make seasoning. Mix soy sauce and cornstarch in a small bowl until smooth. Stir in sesame seed oil, black pepper, and sugar. Set aside.
· Heat 2 tablespoons oil in wok or medium skillet over high heat; stir in garlic, shallots, scallions, ginger, and chili; cook and stir for 1 minute.
· Stir in preserved vegetables, beans, and seasoning sauce; cook and stir 2 minutes or until hot and sauce coats vegetables.
· Transfer to a serving dish.

> **Mind Refresher ❖** Serve with the motivation to
> make others happy—no expectations.

Serves 4

Curry-Seasoned Vegetables

Indian

This recipe comes from a family that ran a guest house in Dehra Dun, in the foothills of the Himalayas. Their simple and clean Indian kitchen had two gas burners, a rack on the wall with stainless steel dishes for both cooking and serving, a table spread with newspaper for cutting vegetables, and a covered container under the counter filled with an assortment of beautiful colored spices. Dishes were washed by hand on the floor in another room. The food was prepared, covered, placed on the table, and eaten when desired. Vegetable dishes were the major part of the meal, and this seasoning method was used over and over. Some other vegetables to try are squash, zucchini, eggplant, mushrooms, green beans, and carrots. The most delicious food came out of this kitchen, and it was served with such graciousness.

METHOD

· Heat oil in medium saucepan over medium-high heat; stir in cumin seeds and cook 1 minute to release flavor.
· Stir in onions and cook, stirring occasionally, 5 minutes or until tender.
· Add tomato, coriander, chili, garam masala, turmeric, and salt; cook, stirring, 2 minutes.
· Stir in potatoes and cauliflower, reduce heat to medium-low, cover, and cook, stirring occasionally, 15 minutes. Add a little water to prevent burning if mixture becomes too dry.
· Stir in frozen peas, cover, and continue cooking 5 minutes or until vegetables are tender.

Mind Refresher ✿ Serve with loving kindness.

Serves 4

2 tablespoons vegetable oil
1 teaspoon cumin seed
¼ medium onion, peeled and diced (about ¼ cup)
1 medium tomato, diced (about ½ cup)
1 teaspoon ground coriander
½ teaspoon chili powder
½ teaspoon ground garam masala (see page 192)
¼ teaspoon ground turmeric
1 teaspoon sea salt
3 medium Yukon gold or white potatoes (12 ounces or 350 g), peeled and cut into 1-inch (2.5-cm) cubes (about 2 cups)
½ medium cauliflower head, cut into bite-size pieces (about 2½ cups)
½ cup (250 g) frozen peas

¼ cup (60 ml) vegetable oil

3 medium Yukon gold or white potatoes (12 ounces or 350 g), peeled and cut french-fry size (about 2½ inches [6.2 cm] long)

6 tablespoons soy sauce

½–¾ cup (125 ml) water

½ teaspoon sea salt

2 tablespoons granulated sugar

2 green onions, sliced diagonally into 1-inch (2.5-cm) pieces

Soy Potatoes with Green Onions

Chinese, from Shanxi Village

Much of the food in this region is either wheat or potatoes. This easy-to-prepare dish is rich and creamy. The potatoes are cut french-fry style and simmered in soy sauce; green onions are added at the end to give color and crunch. It is delicious served with rice and a green vegetable dish.

METHOD

· Heat oil in a Chinese wok or medium skillet over high heat; add potatoes and cook, stirring, 2 minutes or until brown.

Mind Refresher ✿ Stand straight, breathe normally, and concentrate on your breathe for 30 seconds; as distractions come, go back to the breath.

· Stir in soy sauce, water, and salt; reduce heat to low, cover, and cook 10 minutes or until potatoes are tender.
· Mix in sugar and green onions and heat a minute more or until a gravy forms. Add more water for more gravy.

Serves 4

VARIATION

Spicy tomato sauce: Use Roasted Tomato Sauce (see page 135) in place of the water.

Greens with Coconut and Spices

Balinese

Everything that comes out of Bali seems to be soft and sensuous. It is truly an island of the gods. Every morning the people make offering baskets filled with beautiful foods. The baskets are put on trays and taken around the garden compounds. These offerings were seen everywhere, in the streets, in homes, and in restaurant kitchens. The Balinese principle of sharing applies at mealtimes; several dishes are prepared and eaten together with a mound of steamed rice.

This recipe comes from a small hotel kitchen, which was just a room with a burner, a blender, and a grinding mortar and pestle for making spice pastes. In the open-air dining room, you could have a plate of these greens served with rice and tempeh. The flavoring is a delightful combination of a tomato-chili paste called *sambal* (which can be made at home or purchased at Asian markets), lime from kaffir leaves, coconut, and fried shallots.

METHOD

- Make sauce: Blend tomatoes, garlic, chilies, sugar, salt, shallot, nuts, turmeric, and ginger in a blender or food processor 1 minute or until a coarse paste is formed. Heat oil in small skillet over medium heat. Add chili paste and cook, stirring, until it reduces by half. It will be a beautiful red color. Remove from heat and let cool.
- Squeeze out excess water from cooked greens and roughly chop.
- Mix greens, chili paste, coconut, lime juice, and 2 tablespoons fried shallots in a bowl.
- Season with salt. It should be a juicy combination of sweet, sour, salt, and spice.
- Top with remaining fried shallots and serve with steamed rice.

> **Mind Refresher** ❂ Before eating, offer your
> food to all sentient beings
> so that they may never be hungry.

Serves 4

SAMBAL CHILI PASTE

2 medium tomatoes, quartered

4 medium cloves garlic, peeled

2 small fresh green chilies, roughly chopped

1 teaspoon granulated sugar

1 teaspoon sea salt

1 small shallot, peeled and quartered

¼ cup (60 g) candlenuts, cashews, or macadamia nuts

¼ teaspoon ground turmeric or ½ inch (1.2 cm) fresh galangal, peeled and sliced

1-inch (2.5-cm) piece fresh ginger root or kencur, peeled and finely chopped

3 tablespoons vegetable oil

GREENS

3 cups (1 kg) cooked greens (spinach, Swiss chard, or mustard greens), drained of all water, or 2 pounds (1 kg) frozen cut-leaf spinach, thawed

½ cup (125 g) unsweetened shredded coconut

2 tablespoons fresh lime juice or 4 kaffir leaves, shredded

¼ cup (60 g) fried shallots, plus extra for topping

sea salt

Fried Eggplant with Lemon Wedges

North American

2 large eggs, beaten
½ cup (75 g) all-purpose flour
1 large eggplant, with skin, cut
    into ½-inch (1.2-cm) slices
¼ cup (60 ml) vegetable oil
sea salt and freshly ground black
    pepper
lemon wedges

Lightly browned, crispy on the outside, soft in the center, and lightened with a squeeze of lemon, slices of fried eggplant can really hit the spot. It's hard to eat just one slice. My mother used to make them for our family. Serve this dish along with others as part of a meal or make an appetizer of it.

METHOD

Mind Refresher ✿ Appreciate whatever is happening.

· Prepare two shallow dishes, one for eggs and one for flour.
· Coat eggplant slices first with flour, then with egg.
· Heat oil in large skillet over medium heat. Cook eggplant slices 2 minutes or until brown, turn over, and continue cooking until other side is brown and soft.
· Transfer to paper towel–lined plate to drain off excess oil; keep warm until all eggplant slices are cooked, adding more oil as needed.
· Place slices on serving plate, season with salt and pepper, and garnish with lemon wedges.

Serves 4

Doubt and the Egg
A TRUST IN CAUSE, CONDITION, AND EFFECT

In our world today, doubt and criticism are cherished. Devotion and faith are almost an embarrassment, things not to be revealed. Isn't this sad?

You can say devotion and faith are blind, supporting this with all kinds of reasons; you can also use these identical reasons to prove doubt is blind.

Devotion is somewhat difficult to understand. Simply stated, it is trust in cause, condition, and effect. Just that—nothing more! If you want to boil an egg and you have the right causes and conditions—an egg, a saucepan, the right amount of water, heat to boil the water—you trust the water will boil and after some time the egg will be cooked, as long as there is no obstacle, like someone taking the egg out every few seconds. If you have all the right causes and conditions and no obstacles, the egg will be cooked. No choice. That's rational devotion. A cook has confidence, because he has rational devotion.

If you doubt, because of the influence of a society that cherishes doubt, your very intelligent mind will create thousands of reasons why the egg won't cook. You can't even cook an egg without trusting in cause, conditions, and effect.

—DZONGSAR KHYENTSE RINPOCHE

Gourmet Food

Karma is what makes you interpret. When you have good karma, a phenomenon that might be considered painful by another could be interpreted by you as pleasurable, or at least it would not bother you.

Now, the Buddha is an all-accomplished being. Thus it is believed that even if not a single being were remaining on this earth and the Buddha were to beg alms, all he would need do is hold out his begging bowl into empty space and there would be gods ready to offer whatever he wished.

But on one particular occasion, because the Buddha Shakyamuni wanted to teach the monks something about the interpretation of mind, he went along to Kosala. He and Ananda and all the monks continued going up and down begging for some time, and still no one had offered a thing.

Finally, late one morning, the king's men in charge of the stables offered the horses' leftovers to the monks and the Buddha. The monks felt disgusted, yet not being allowed to eat after midday, they had no choice but to eat these offerings. So they ate, and the Buddha also ate, and all the monks felt really bad. They felt sick and revolted. Then the Buddha asked, "Isn't the lunch delicious?" And then, of course, the monks complained. But when they tried the leftovers from the Buddha's bowl, although it was the very same thing, it was like eating gourmet food of the god realms. This is what it's like. Different beings have different karma. The Buddha was teaching karmic interpretation.

—DZONGSAR KHYENTSE RINPOCHE

CHAPTER 6

Condiments, Spreads, and Sauces

for Tasting the Moment

Love and Refrigerator

I had been living with an Asian guy for seven months and was completely in love. He cooked all his favorite dishes for me; everything he did was wonderful, new, exciting, and different. I loved his cooking and him.

Then one day, I returned home from shopping in the market with a basket full of food. I opened the refrigerator and saw it was jam-packed with all his food and condiments. It was the first time I noticed them, and I thought, "What is all this foreign stuff in my refrigerator? Ugh!" What was once exciting and exotic had become irritating. My fickle mind changed, my perception changed. I began to wonder if this was the beginning of the end of my love story.

— **MARIA LOPEZ,** *Spanish*

Condiments

~~~~~~~~~~~~~~~~~~~~~~~~~~~~~~~

Condiments are used to add interest to meals by providing a wide range of flavors and textures. In Eastern cuisines, flavors are combined not only to make complex and satisfying tastes but also to aid digestion, encouraging the release of enzymes that break down nutrients. The different flavors are bitter (coffee, bitter chocolate, radishes), sour (lemon, vinegar, apples), salty (olives, parsley, seaweed), pungent/spicy (ginger, cayenne, garlic), and sweet (honey, maple syrup, bananas). Serve condiments in little bowls at the center of the table for everyone to take a little bit. It's also nice to have bowls of olives, pickles, peppers, and soy sauce, depending on the meal. Here are some condiment recipes; note that you can also find delicious prepared ones in markets.

1 medium cucumber, peeled,
    halved, seeded, and thinly
    sliced (about 1½ cups)
1 cup (250 g) cottage cheese
¼–1 teaspoon red chili powder,
    according to taste
2 green onions, thinly sliced
    (about ½ cup)
1 medium tomato, diced (about
    ½ cup)
½ bunch fresh cilantro leaves,
    chopped (about ½ cup)
½ teaspoon sea salt

Chili-Flavored Cottage Cheese

Bhutanese

The Bhutanese like their food spicy and so use lots of chilies and chili powder for flavoring. It is not uncommon to see them leaving the market with three to four pounds of chilies for the week. Their cheese is usually made from yak milk. A Bhutanese meal is a plate full of rice served with little side dishes, all eaten with the hands. With its yummy blend of flavors—cucumber, tomato, and chili—this dish is also good as a topping for baked potatoes.

METHOD

> **Mind Refresher** ✿ **Stand straight, breath normally, and watch the moment's breath for 30 seconds.**

· Mix cucumber, cottage cheese, chili powder, onions, tomato, cilantro, and salt in a small bowl, or for a smooth texture, blend in a food processor.
· Transfer to serving dish.

Makes 1½ cups (350 g)

1 medium cucumber, peeled,
    seeded, and diced (about
    1½ cups)
¼ teaspoon sea salt
1 cup (250 g) plain yogurt
¼ medium onion, peeled and
    diced (about ½ cup)
1 clove garlic, peeled and finely
    chopped
1 tablespoon finely chopped
    fresh mint
sea salt and freshly ground black
    pepper

Tart Cucumber Yogurt Sauce

Turkish, from Istanbul

In Istanbul, cucumber sauce is served as an accompaniment to meals. It is also eaten as a snack with special pita bread, a large round loaf from which pieces are pulled to eat. This condiment has a sour, pungent flavor. The yogurt aids digestion and gives some protein. Buy a good-quality organic yogurt, or try making your own (see page 191). A high-quality yogurt has a natural culture.

METHOD

· Mix cucumber and salt in a bowl; let sit 30 minutes to draw out water.

> **Mind Refresher** ✿ As you squeeze cucumber, stand straight, relax, and breathe normally; watch your hand squeezing the cucumber— concentrate on it for 30 seconds.

· Squeeze out extra moisture from cucumber and drain off liquid.
· Return cucumber to bowl; mix in yogurt, onion, garlic, and mint.
· Season with salt and pepper.
· Transfer to a serving bowl.

Makes 1½ cups (250 g)

VARIATIONS

Cumin chili yogurt: To cucumber and yogurt, add ½ teaspoon cumin powder; 1 small green chili, seeded and finely chopped; and 1 tablespoon ground coriander.

Nut chili cilantro yogurt: To cucumber and yogurt, add ½ cup (60 g) finely chopped cashews or almonds; 1 small green chili, seeded and finely chopped; and 1 tablespoon finely chopped fresh cilantro leaves.

Mint-raisin yogurt: To cucumber and yogurt, add 2 tablespoons finely chopped fresh mint leaves; 2 tablespoons raisins, soaked; and 1 tablespoon finely chopped walnuts.

Red Tomato-Chili Salsa

Mexican

This multipurpose condiment can be found in every Mexican kitchen. A basic crowd pleaser on its own, as the popularity of corn tortilla chips and salsa attests, it can also be mixed with black beans or pinto beans to create another dip. Use as many chiles as suit your taste.

METHOD

- Mix tomatoes, onions, chilies, and cilantro in a small bowl.
- Add water and season with salt.

> **Mind Refresher** ✿ Stand straight, breathe normally, and watch the moment's mind as you appreciate the colors and textures of the salsa.

- Transfer to a serving dish. Serve within 3 hours (it will lose its crispness after that).

Makes 1½ cups (350 g)

VARIATIONS

Indian flavor: To above ingredients add diced cucumber, lemon juice, and a pinch sugar.

Bhutanese flavor: To above ingredients add feta or cottage cheese.

2 medium tomatoes, diced (about 1 cup)
½ medium onion, peeled and diced
1–2 serrano chilies or any fresh chilies, finely chopped
generous handful finely chopped fresh cilantro leaves (about ¼ cup)
¼ cup (60 ml) water
sea salt

Spicy Soy-Sauced Tomatoes

Indonesian

Condiments in Indonesian cooking are just as important as the savory dishes they are served with. Meals come with a small platter of three or four different, flavored, textured, and colored sambals (condiments) to taste. The soy sauce in this condiment gives it a salty flavor, with pungent and sour notes.

METHOD

Mind Refresher ✿ Stand straight, relax, and breathe normally; appreciate whatever is happening.

- Mix tomatoes, chilies, shallots, soy sauce, lemon juice, and basil in a bowl.
- Serve as a condiment.

Makes 1 cup (250 g)

2 medium tomatoes, cut in half and sliced (about 1 cup)

2 small Thai or serrano red or green chilies, seeded and thinly sliced (use to taste)

2 small shallots or ¼ onion, peeled and thinly sliced (about ¼ cup)

2 tablespoons soy sauce

3 tablespoons fresh lemon juice

1 tablespoon finely chopped fresh basil or fresh cilantro leaves

1 cup (150 g) sunflower seeds
2 tablespoons tamari or soy sauce

Toasted Tamari Sunflower Seeds

Australian

These are good to have on the table as well as to keep by the stove, along with Indonesian fried shallots. Add a sprinkle here and there to give dishes a crunchy texture. Packets of deep-fried shallots are generally available in Asian stores. If the packets lose their crispness, put them in the oven on low heat and then let them cool. A pile of the shallots and these seeds on top of a plate of steamed greens is wonderful. Also try making a combination of seeds—sunflower, pumpkin, flax, and sesame.

METHOD

> **Mind Refresher** ✿ Stand straight, breathe normally, and breathe in and out 3 times; as the mind wanders, bring it back to the breath.

· Roast seeds in a dry medium skillet over medium heat until lightly browned.
· Remove from heat and stir in tamari.
· Transfer to a container and store.

Makes 1 cup (150 g)

1 tablespoon coarse sea salt

1 cup (150 g) sesame seeds

¼ cup (15 g) wakame (optional),
roasted in dry skillet

Crunchy Sesame Flavoring/Gomashio

Japanese

This salty all-purpose condiment works well with many dishes. In addition to providing some protein and calcium, it gives a special touch to rice and salads. Try grinding dried wakame or other seaweeds and dried herbs into it. A nutritious herb to try might be dried nettles (see page 180), since the combination of nettles and seaweeds is chock-full of minerals. Try also combining black and white sesame seeds with flax seeds.

METHOD

· Roast salt in a dry medium skillet over medium heat, 1 minute or until it begins to release a smell.
· In a suribachi (Japanese mortar and pestle) grind salt to a fine powder and set aside. An ordinary mortar and pestle will also work.
· Roast sesame seeds in a dry skillet, covered, over medium heat, shaking until they pop and are brown.

Mind Refresher ❂ Stand straight, breathe normally,
and focus on the grinding of the sesame seeds;
as your thoughts wander,
keep returning your attention to the seeds.

· Transfer sesame seeds to the suribachi and grind until two-thirds are crushed.
· Mix sesame seeds and salt.
· Keep in a jar and use with meals.

Makes 1 cup (150 g)

COOKING SUGGESTIONS

Marinating tofu: Cut tofu into strips and marinate with olive oil, tamari, and gomashio.

Stir-fried vegetables: Mix gomashio with a little tamari and oil as a seasoning for your stir-fry.

Seasonal Fruit Chutney

Indian

In Indian cuisine, two or three different condiments are served at the table—pungent (spicy), sweet, and sour—to enhance the flavors of the meal. Make this sweet and pungent chutney with seasonal fruits. The candied ginger can be found in specialty stores or in the Asian sections of good supermarkets.

METHOD

· Mix peaches, sugar, vinegar, raisins, ginger, onion, garlic, mustard seed, chili powder, and salt in a heavy 3-quart (3-L) pot. Bring to a boil, uncovered, over high heat.

> **Mind Refresher** ✿ Stand straight, relax, and breathe normally; appreciate the aromas.

· Reduce heat to medium-low and cook, stirring occasionally, 1 hour or until thick and fruit is glazed.
· Pour into hot sterilized canning jars and seal immediately.
· Fill a large pot three-quarters full with water and bring to a boil.
· Place jars in boiling water for 5 minutes. Water should cover jars completely.
· Remove jars from water and turn upside down on a towel to cool; this seals jars.

Makes 6 half-pints (250 ml)

4 pounds (2 kg) peaches, pears, or other fruit, peeled and cut into 1-inch (2.5-cm) pieces (about 7 cups)
1½ cups (350 g) light brown sugar
2 cups (500 ml) apple cider vinegar
1 cup (175 g) raisins
⅔ cup (150 g) finely chopped candied ginger
1 medium onion, diced (about 1 cup)
1 clove garlic, peeled and finely chopped
2 tablespoons mustard seed
1 tablespoon chili powder
1 tablespoon sea salt

Spreads

~~~~~~~~~~~~~~~~

Roasted Red Pepper and Garlic Hummus
Middle Eastern

The origins of hummus are Middle Eastern, but this particular recipe comes from the state of Nevada. It's the roasted garlic that makes this spread so creamy and addictive, as well as a boost to your immune system. Roasted peppers are also heavenly. Garbanzo beans or chickpeas are hard dry peas, about half an inch in diameter, with a nut-like flavor. They come in cans or can be purchased dry in bulk. If you use dry ones, soak them for eight hours first and then cook them for two to three hours. Serve this spread on all things. Bagels are a favorite. It also makes a delicious base on sandwiches instead of mayonnaise. Or try it as an alternative to butter on toast.

2 medium garlic heads, tops
    cut off
1 can (15 ounces or 450 g)
    garbanzo beans, drained and
    rinsed
½ cup (125 g) roasted red bell
    peppers, roughly chopped
2 tablespoons fresh lemon juice
1 tablespoon tahini
¼ cup (60 ml) water
¼ cup (60 ml) olive oil
1 teaspoon ground cumin
¼ teaspoon ground cayenne
½ teaspoon sea salt

METHOD

· Preheat oven to 400° F (200° C).
· Put garlic heads in a small baking dish, cover, and roast 45 minutes or until soft.

> **Mind Refresher** ✿ Stand straight, relax, and breathe normally; watch the present-moment mind for 30 seconds.

· Squeeze roasted cloves out of their skins into a small bowl.
· Blend garlic, beans, peppers, lemon juice, tahini, water, oil, cumin, cayenne and salt in a blender or food processor until smooth and creamy.
· Adjust consistency with water.

Makes 1 ½ cups (350 g)

ROASTED RED PEPPERS

Place peppers directly on stove flame or under broiler and char on all sides. Put charred peppers in a plastic bag to sweat 15 minutes. Peel off skins under running water. Remove cores, seeds, and white veins before roughly chopping.

1 medium-ripe avocado, peeled,
    pitted, and halved
4 ounces (125 g) firm tofu,
    crumbled
1 rib celery, finely chopped (about
    ½ cup)
2 tablespoons fresh lemon juice
2 tablespoons finely chopped
    fresh ginger root
2 tablespoons tamari or soy sauce
1 clove garlic, finely chopped
¼ teaspoon sea salt
⅛ teaspoon ground cayenne

Gingery Tofu-Avocado Spread

North American, from California

The combination of tofu and avocado with the spiciness of ginger and the lightness of lemon makes for an unusual flavor blend. This delicious dish can be used as a spread or served on a bed of lettuce as a meal, accompanied by other little salads, such as shredded carrots and cooked beets.

METHOD

> **Mind Refresher** ✿ Stand straight, breathe normally, and be present as you mash the avocado; keep returning to this process as the mind wanders.

- With the back of a fork, mash avocado in a medium bowl until chunky.
- Using fork, stir in tofu, celery, lemon juice, ginger, tamari, garlic, salt, and cayenne until mixed but not smooth. Do not use a blender because the mixture should be textured.
- Transfer to a serving bowl.

Makes about 1 cup (250 g)

Classic Textured Guacamole

Mexican

Guacamole makes a flavorful condiment with a meal, a tasty dip for tortilla chips or raw vegetables, and a succulent salad on a bed of lettuce. It is also good on bagels or other breads with a sprinkle of chopped green onions on top. Use cooked broccoli with a little oil instead of avocados and you could call it broccomoli. Or try mixing the two. Sun-dried tomatoes make a nice addition too.

METHOD

· Peel avocados, cut them in half, and remove stones; set aside one stone.
· Scoop out flesh and put in a small mixing bowl.

Mind Refresher ✿ Stand straight, breathe normally, and watch your breath for 30 seconds.

· Mash avocado flesh with the back of a fork until somewhat smooth but still chunky. Do not use a blender because that would make it too smooth.
· Mix in tomatoes, onions, lemon juice, chilies, cilantro, and salt.
· Transfer to serving dish and put the saved stone in the center—this prevents guacamole from turning brown—until serving time.

Makes 1½ cups (350 g)

2 medium-ripe avocados
1 medium tomato, diced (about ½ cup)
½ onion, peeled and diced (about ½ cup)
2 tablespoons fresh lemon juice
1–2 small serrano chilies, finely chopped, or ½ teaspoon ground cayenne
1 tablespoon chopped fresh cilantro leaves
sea salt

2 pounds (1 kg) fresh strawberries
4 cups (1 kg) granulated sugar
¼ cup (125 ml) fresh lemon juice
    (about 2 lemons)

Fresh Strawberry Jam

English

Strawberry jam is everyone's favorite, especially children's. My children loved it spread on slices of cheddar cheese (a Brazilian snack). You can make it from spring through summer. Since it is a looser kind of jam, try it stirred into yogurt, over ice cream, or in banana-split sundaes (sliced bananas, ice cream, strawberry sauce, caramel sauce, and chocolate sauce, topped with whipped cream and toasted nuts). Or simply enjoy the old favorite: a good slice of bread, butter, and jam, served with a cup of tea.

METHOD

· Rinse the strawberries and remove the hulls.

> **Mind Refresher** ✿ Stand straight, breathe normally,
> put a strawberry in your mouth, and taste it.
> Let go of labels as they come up
> and return to the taste experience.

· Place strawberries in a heavy 3-quart (3-L) pot, crushing a few berries near the base of the pot. Cook over low heat 25 minutes or until fruit is soft and juices run.
· Stir in sugar and cook, stirring, until sugar dissolves.
· Stir in lemon juice, turn up heat to high, and bring to a boil. Cook rapidly 20 minutes or until setting point is reached—when a drop holds firm left on a cold plate. Stir only to prevent sticking.
· Remove pot from heat and let cool at least 30 minutes or until the jam is just warm. This distributes berries evenly throughout the jam.
· Stir gently and pour jam into hot sterilized canning jars. Cover and seal immediately. Turn jars upside down on a towel to cool. Label when cold.

Makes 5 half-pints (250 ml)

Harvest Apple Butter

European

7 large apples (1 kg), peeled,
cored, and cut into chunks
(about 7 cups)

Apples remind us that fall is here and summer has ended. Cooking gives them a buttery consistency and a rich color. This jam is delicious on toast or pancakes; it also makes a nice dessert mixed with plain yogurt and topped with chopped walnuts and a sprinkle of cinnamon.

METHOD

Mind Refresher ✿ Stand straight, relax, and breathe normally. Watch the present moment's mind for 30 seconds; as your thoughts run here and there, keep returning to the breath.

· Put apples in a heavy 3-quart (3-L) pot over low heat. Cover and cook, stirring occasionally to prevent sticking, 1–1½ hours or until buttery smooth; add a little water if it begins to stick. Use a flame tamer to prevent burning.
· Transfer to a storage container. Allowing butter to sit awhile enhances its flavor.

Makes about 3 cups (750 g)

16 ounces (175 g) fresh basil
(about 4 packed cups)
½–1 cup (125–250 ml) virgin
olive oil
¼ cup (30 g) pine nuts, almonds,
or walnuts (or a combination)
3–4 cloves garlic, peeled
3 tablespoons grated fresh
Parmesan cheese
½ teaspoon sea salt
¼ teaspoon freshly ground
black pepper

Green Basil Pesto

Italian and North American

Basil has a fresh, clovelike fragrance and a spicy taste. This highly aromatic herb grows one- to three-feet tall, has pale green, glossy leaves, and comes to full bloom at the end of summer. It is easy to grow in your garden. Dried and mixed with lemon verbena and oregano, it makes a nice digestive tea. But much of basil's fame and popularity can be attributed to its use in pesto. People love spreading this green garlicky sauce on almost everything. Pesto mixed with mayonnaise or heavy cream makes a good topping for grilled eggplant.

METHOD

Mind Refresher ✿ Stand straight, breathe normally, and take in the aroma of the basil; concentrate on this aroma for 30 seconds, bringing the mind back when it wanders.

- Remove stocks from basil plants and measure 4 packed cups.
- Put half the leaves in a blender or a food processor; add ½ cup (125 ml) oil and blend, gradually adding remaining basil.
- Add nuts, garlic, cheese, salt, and pepper; blend to desired consistency, adding more oil as needed.
- Toss pesto with pasta of your choice or keep refrigerated for later use.

Makes about 1½ cups (350 g)

VARIATIONS

Red pepper pesto: Use roasted red bell peppers, toasted pumpkin seeds, basil (smaller amount), olive oil, and garlic.

Nondairy pesto: Use dill, cilantro, or basil, a nut butter, silken tofu instead of cheese, olive oil, and lemon juice.

Sun-dried tomato pesto: Use one third each sun-dried tomatoes, basil, and flat-leaf parsley, plus olive oil, nuts, cheese, and garlic.

White Béchamel Sauce

French

4 tablespoons (60 g) butter
¼ cup (45 g) all-purpose flour
2 cups (500 ml) milk
sea salt and white pepper
pinch ground nutmeg

In classic French cooking, many sauces begin with this white-sauce base. It can be varied by adding curry powder, cheese, onions, mushrooms, herbs, tomato paste, or broth. This sauce is perfect poured over broccoli, cauliflower, or spinach in a baked gratin, as a soothing cheese sauce mixed with pasta, or as a mushroom or fresh herb sauce over fried tofu and rice. Also try it as a chipotle chili cream sauce.

METHOD

· Melt butter in a heavy saucepan over medium heat; stir in flour and cook 1 minute.

> **Mind Refresher** ✿ Stand straight, relax, and breathe normally. Watch your in-and-out breaths for 30 seconds; as your mind wanders, keep bringing it back to the breath.

· With a wire whisk, gradually whisk in milk until mixture is smooth and has no lumps. If there are lumps, strain through a sieve.
· Season to taste with salt, pepper, and nutmeg. Add other flavorings as desired.
· Bring to a boil, reduce heat to low, and cook, stirring, 10 minutes or until sauce thickens.

Makes 1½ cups (350 ml)

½ cup (125 g) chunky peanut
   butter, tahini, or cashew butter
½ cup (125 ml) hot water or
   coconut milk
¼ cup chopped onion
1 tablespoon honey
1 tablespoon lime or lemon juice
2 teaspoons tamari or soy sauce
1 teaspoon finely chopped fresh
   ginger root
¼ teaspoon ground cumin
⅛ teaspoon ground cayenne or
   a finely chopped small fresh
   chili pepper

Creamy Peanut Sauce

Australian and Indonesian

In Indonesia you can order a plate of steamed seasonal vegetables with this sauce on the side for dipping. The traditional version uses peanuts as its base; in Australia they use tahini and cashew butters. It is delicious on Chinese noodles, baked potatoes, shredded vegetable tofu salad, or just rice topped with fried shallots (see page 190) or chopped green onions.

METHOD

Mind Refresher ✿ Stand straight, breathe normally, and taste the nut butter. Concentrate on the taste in your mouth, returning to it when your mind wanders.

· Blend all ingredients in an electric blender or food processor until smooth, adding more liquid as needed.

Makes ½ cup (125 g)

Roasted Tomato Sauce

Mexican

2 medium whole tomatoes
1 small, whole, green or red
    serrano or other chili
½ medium onion, with skin
2 cloves garlic, with skin
1 tablespoon vegetable oil
¼ teaspoon sea salt

This is an excellent sauce over pasta, rice, potatoes, tofu, or eggs. The key to its earthy color and taste is roasting the tomatoes, chili, onion, and garlic before blending them. In Mexico the vegetables are roasted on a flat skillet over an open fire until charred.

METHOD

- Roast tomatoes, chili, onion, and garlic cloves in a dry medium skillet over medium-high heat or under the broiler, turning occasionally, until tomatoes become soft and vegetables char.
- Remove skins from onion and garlic.
- Put vegetables in an electric blender or food processor and blend until smooth.

> **Mind Refresher** ✿ **Stand straight, relax, and breath normally. Appreciate whatever is happening.**

- Heat oil in skillet over medium-low heat; add vegetable blend and cook, uncovered, stirring, 10 minutes or until sauce begins to darken.

Makes 1 cup (250 ml)

SUGGESTIONS

Tomato soup: Use the sauce as a base; add carrot, corn, zucchini, and vegetable broth; simmer 20 minutes. Serve garnished with corn tortilla strips.

Sauce over tofu: Fry a tofu cutlet, add sauce, and garnish with shredded cabbage, cilantro, and feta.

½ cup (150 g) red lentils

2 tablespoons olive oil

1 medium onion, diced (about
1 cup)

1 medium carrot, diced (about
1 cup)

2 medium celery ribs with leaves,
diced (about 1 cup)

generous handful finely chopped
fresh herbs (rosemary, thyme,
basil, oregano) (about ¼ cup)
or 1 teaspoon dried oregano

2 cloves garlic, peeled and finely
chopped

1 can (14½ ounces) peeled
and diced tomatoes or 4 fresh
tomatoes, peeled and diced
(about 2 cups)

2 cups (500 ml) water

½ teaspoon sea salt

¼ teaspoon freshly ground black
pepper

Red Lentil Bolognese Sauce

Italian and Indian

Red lentils, popular in Indian cuisine, give substance as well as protein to a classic tomato sauce. Serve this sauce over pasta, rice, potatoes, or tofu. Kids might prefer it blended—they usually hate chunky things.

METHOD

· Cover lentils with water. Soak 10 minutes, drain in a colander, rinse twice, and set aside.

· Heat oil in large nonstick skillet over medium heat; add onion and cook, stirring occasionally, until soft.

Mind Refresher ✿ **Stand straight, breathe normally, and watch the mind's thoughts for 30 seconds— nothing else to do.**

· Stir in carrots, celery, herbs, and garlic; cook, stirring, 5 minutes.

· Add lentils, tomatoes with their juice, water, salt, and pepper; bring to a boil over high heat.

· Reduce heat to low, cover, and cook, stirring occasionally, 45 minutes or until lentils are cooked.

Makes 2 cups (500 g)

Satisfaction Guaranteed

When we are hungry, reading a cookbook won't help.
We endlessly collect recipes
To imagine what they'd taste like.
We want the delight of that first bite
Then the thrill is over and on to the next recipe.
This mind of ours is forever hungry.
Taste the fresh moment's mind,
Served, eaten, and digested daily,
Satisfaction guaranteed.

Refresher Sessions

Our Fresh Mind meditation sessions are just as important in our lives
as three meals a day, plus snacks.

—JIGME KHYENTSE RINPOCHE

CHAPTER 7

Desserts

for Serving Generosity

The Shopping Story

There are many skillful ways to live our lives, to be less selfish and less attached. I learned one of these ways when I was a new student of Chagdud Tulku Rinpoche, Tibetan Buddhist master, in Oregon, and I took him to the grocery store. I had lots to do, so I ran into the store and got the shopping cart. I was halfway down the aisle before I looked around and realized I didn't know where Rinpoche was. I thought, "Oh my God, I have lost the lama!" I began backtracking. There he was standing at the front door—he had just come in and hadn't moved two steps from the front door.

I went over to him and whispered in his ear, "Psst, psst! What are you doing?"

Rinpoche said, "I am offering, I am offering. Look at these shelves, look at the food, look at all this stuff."

I said, "It is not yours."

"Yes, it is mine," he replied. "My eyes see it. It is part of my world. It is mine to offer. Offering to all the Buddhas and bodhisattvas, to all the sentient beings, so that they may receive all this food, they may receive all that is on these shelves, that they may never be hungry."

— LAMA TSERING EVEREST, *American*

Desserts are always fun to prepare, especially on weekends or holidays, when there is more time. Every family has its favorites. The simplest and best are fresh seasonal fruit, which bursts with flavor. Avoid the tasteless imported fruit found in most supermarkets and instead shop at farmers' markets and natural food stores. Look for strawberries in spring and cherries in early summer. Summer brings its crop of apricots, peaches, melons, raspberries, and blueberries, while fall offers pears, apples, and plums. Freeze fresh fruit in summer to enjoy in the colder months, when citrus fruits and kiwis are also available. Dried fruit makes a satisfying after-meal treat. The French sometimes serve a bowl of nuts after a meal, before coffee. Packaged nuts cannot compare in flavor to freshly cracked walnuts, almonds, hazelnuts, or pecans. And do not neglect that old standby, a piece of good-quality dark chocolate, which always finishes a meal perfectly.

1 cup (150 g) black sesame seeds
1¼ cups (300 ml) whole milk
1 cup (225 g) granulated sugar
1 large organic egg
1 rounded tablespoon peanut butter
½ teaspoon vanilla extract
1¾ cups (400 ml) heavy cream

Black Sesame Ice Cream

Chinese, from Hong Kong

This delicious nutty-flavored ice cream is easy to make. Black sesame seeds can be found in Asian markets; if you can't find them, use white sesame seeds. Try this and the ginger ice cream (see page 142), and then you can start creating your own recipes. Both of these ice creams were made for charity benefits in Hong Kong; the woman who gave me the recipes had a repertoire of over sixty recipes.

METHOD

· Roast sesame seeds in a dry skillet over medium heat, covered, until they pop.

> **Mind Refresher ✿** Stand straight, breathe normally, and focus your awareness on grinding the sesame seeds; as your mind wanders, come back to this process.

· Grind sesame seeds with a mortar and pestle or in coffee grinder until powdered.
· Blend sesame-seed powder, milk, sugar, egg, peanut butter, and vanilla in an electric blender or food processor until smooth.
· Add heavy cream and blend one more minute.
· Refrigerate 12 hours or overnight.
· Churn in an electric ice-cream maker 20–25 minutes or until ice-cream consistency. Freeze until ready to serve.

Makes 3 cups (750 g)

1½ cups (350 ml) whole milk

3 large organic eggs

1½ tablespoons ground ginger

1 cup (225 g) granulated sugar

2 cups (480 ml) heavy cream

1 teaspoon finely chopped fresh ginger root or 1 tablespoon finely chopped crystallized ginger

1 teaspoon ginger juice (see page 193)

Ginger Ice Cream

Chinese, from Hong Kong

The ginger in this recipe aids the digestion of the ice cream; ginger has a warming nature that changes the cold nature of the ice cream, so the stomach isn't trying to digest something completely cold. Try serving this ice cream with a chocolate sauce, candied ginger, and sugared walnuts for a special sundae treat.

METHOD

Mind Refresher ✿ Stand straight, relax, and breathe normally; focus on the breath for 30 seconds, with no regret as thoughts come—just return to the breath.

· Blend milk, eggs, ground ginger, and sugar in an electric blender or food processor until smooth.
· Add heavy cream and blend one more minute.
· Refrigerate 12 hours or overnight.
· Stir in fresh ginger and ginger juice.
· Churn in an electric ice-cream maker for 20–25 minutes or until ice-cream consistency. Freeze until ready to serve.

Makes 3 cups (750 g)

IF YOU DON'T HAVE AN ICE-CREAM MAKER

Pour the preparation into a stainless steel bowl (stainless steel is a good conductor of cold). Put the bowl in the freezer for one hour. Blend the mixture with a hand mixer. Put the bowl back in the freezer for another hour. Repeat this mixing and freezing procedure two times. Then return the bowl to the freezer until you are ready to serve the ice cream.

Sweet Potato Rum Cake

French Caribbean

When one thinks of the Caribbean, one thinks of color, music, and fun. This cake could be found at a carnival or on a French table for dessert. It has a delectable aroma of sweet potatoes blended with vanilla, cinnamon, and delicious dark rum. Baked in a loaf pan with a toasted-coconut crust, the cake is moist when sliced but light and full of flavor for the fall and winter months.

METHOD

- Preheat oven to 400° F (200° C).
- Butter all sides of a 9 x 5 x 3–inch (23 x 13 x 6–cm) loaf pan.
- Bake potatoes on oven rack 45 minutes or until soft.
- Peel potatoes and blend them in an electric blender or food processor until smooth.

Mind Refresher ✿ As you beat the eggs, stand straight, breathe normally, and watch your breath.

- Beat eggs and sugar in a medium mixing bowl until mixture is a light lemon color.
- Stir in butter, rum, cinnamon, vanilla extract, and blended potatoes; mix well.
- Pour batter into buttered loaf pan.
- Bake, uncovered, 50 minutes; remove, cover top with coconut, and bake 10 minutes more or until a knife inserted comes out clean and coconut is lightly browned; remove pan from oven and let cool.
- Slice and serve. Refrigerate overnight for firmer texture.

Serves 6–8

butter for preparing pan
4 medium sweet potatoes
(2 pounds or 1 kg)
2 large eggs
1 cup (200 g) light brown sugar
¾ cup (6 ounces or 75 g) butter, melted
3 tablespoons dark rum
1 tablespoon ground cinnamon
1 teaspoon vanilla extract
½ cup (40 g) shredded unsweetened coconut

Sweet and Tart Pineapple Fritters

Vietnamese

These pineapple fritters, crisp and tart, are served piping hot sprinkled with sugar, toasted sesame seeds, and a sprinkle of rum or rice wine. Other fruits, such as bananas or apples, may also be used. The secret to good fritters is making sure your oil is fresh (use peanut, sunflower, grape-seed, or cottonseed oil; old oil becomes foamy when heated and has an acrid smell) and the cooking temperature is high enough. Prepared under these conditions, these fritters are delicious.

METHOD

· Dry pineapple slices between paper towels.
· Prepare the batter: Stir together flour, cornstarch, sugar, and
    baking powder in a small bowl. Mix in water slowly until smooth.
    Refrigerate 20 minutes.
· Heat 3 inches (7.5 cm) of oil in a skillet or wok to 360° F (185° C) or
    until dough dropped in comes back up.
· Coat pineapple rings with batter and slide into oil.
· Cook rings 2 minutes on each side or until browned.
· Take out with slotted spoon and drain on a paper-lined plate.
· Continue cooking rings until all are cooked. Test for heat level
    between each batch.
· Serve immediately, sprinkled with wine, sugar, and sesame seeds.

> **Mind Refresher** ✿ Serve the fritters with kindness and
> the motivation to bring happiness to others.

Makes 8 fritters

8–10 slices pineapple, canned
    or fresh
2–3 tablespoons rice wine or
    rum (optional)
2 tablespoon sesame seeds,
    toasted
3 tablespoons confectioner's
    sugar
4 cups (1 L) frying oil

BATTER
1 cup (150 g) all-purpose flour
⅓ cup (75 g) cornstarch
1 teaspoon granulated sugar
1 teaspoon baking powder
1 cup (250 ml) tepid water

butter and flour for preparing pan

6 ounces (125 g) dark chocolate (70 percent cocoa)

½ cup (4 ounces or 125 g) unsalted butter

½ cup (125 g) confectioner's sugar

4 large eggs, separated

2 tablespoons (30 g) all-purpose flour

pinch salt

CHOCOLATE GLAZE

6 ounces (125 g) dark chocolate (70 percent cocoa)

¼ cup (2 ounces or 65 g) unsalted butter

Gâteau Jinette

French

This recipe was a French family favorite. It was handed down through the generations, beginning with a great-aunt, whose cook created it. The French love chocolate—it is an obsession. They serve a piece of chocolate with coffee after meals or at any time of day in a café with an espresso. At Christmas the stores are filled with it. This simple cake is not too sweet. It is light and richly flavored. Use a high-quality dark chocolate (70-plus percent cocoa) to achieve the best taste. Baked in a round cake pan and spread with a chocolate glaze, it is a perfect dessert that will please a chocolate lover—for birthday celebrations, with tea or coffee, or as an ending to dinners. For a different *goût,* try perfuming with coffee or orange.

METHOD

- Preheat oven to 350°F (180°C).
- Butter and lightly dust with flour an 8-inch (20-cm) round cake pan.
- Melt chocolate and butter in small saucepan in a water bath over medium heat (or put saucepan in a skillet with simmering water).
- Pour into a medium mixing bowl to cool slightly.
- Put sugar through a sieve and sprinkle into melted chocolate.
- Whisk sugar and yolks together into cooled chocolate, until blended.
- Whisk in flour.
- Beat egg whites with pinch salt until they form stiff peaks.
- Fold chocolate mixture slowly into egg whites by cutting vertically through the mixture and then sliding the spatula across the bottom of the bowl and up the side, turning the mixture over until all is lightly blended, like a mousse.
- Pour batter into cake pan and spread evenly.
- Bake 30–35 minutes.

CHOCOLATE GLAZE

- Melt chocolate and butter in a small saucepan in a water bath.
- Insert knife into cake. The cake is done when there is little chocolate stuck to it. Take out and spread with chocolate glaze while still warm. Cool.

> **Mind Refresher** ✿ As you eat the chocolate cake, savor the moment.

Serves 6–8

Light Pumpkin Chiffon Pie

North American

This classic American pie is served in November for Thanksgiving, the holiday for giving thanks. Full of pumpkin spice flavor and topped with whipped cream, this version differs from the typical pumpkin pie in that it has added egg whites, which give it a light texture. A ready-made piecrust makes it easier to prepare; with no mess and no fuss, the pie is finished in no time.

METHOD

> **Mind Refresher** ✿ Make a prayer offering to all sentient beings that they may have causes and conditions for happiness and prosperity and always food to be nourished by.

- Mix pumpkin, milk, egg yolks, gelatin, ½ cup (110 g) sugar, salt, cinnamon, allspice, ginger, and nutmeg in a medium saucepan over medium heat; cook, stirring, 5 minutes.
- Pour into a medium bowl and let cool partially in the refrigerator to thicken slightly.
- Beat egg whites with pinch salt. When they begin to form peaks, stir in ¼ cup (55 g) sugar and beat until they hold stiff peaks.
- Fold egg whites and whipped heavy cream in thirds into cooled pumpkin mixture.
- Pour into baked pie shell. Cover and refrigerate until firm.
- Spread whipped cream on firm pie.
- Cut into wedges and serve.

Serves 6–8

1 cup (250 g) canned pumpkin puree
¾ cup (175 g) whole milk
2 egg yolks, slightly beaten
1 envelope (¼ ounce, 1 tablespoon, or 8 g) unflavored gelatin
¾ cup (165 g) granulated sugar (½ cup [100 g] and ¼ cup [55 g])
½ teaspoon sea salt
½ teaspoon ground cinnamon
½ teaspoon ground allspice
¼ teaspoon ground ginger
¼ teaspoon ground nutmeg
2 egg whites
½ cup (125 ml) heavy cream, whipped
1 baked piecrust, 9–10 inches
1 cup (250 g) whipped cream

1 cup (125 g) quick-cooking oats

1 cup (150 g) all-purpose flour

¾ cup (175 g) light brown sugar or
    raw sugar

1 teaspoon ground cinnamon

¼ teaspoon sea salt

4 ounces butter, cut into ½-inch
    (1.2-cm) cubes

6–8 green apples (2 pounds or
    1 kg), with skins and coarsely
    chopped (about 6 cups)

1 cup (250 g) frozen raspberries
    (optional)

½ cup (125 ml) water or apple
    juice

Fresh Fruit Crisp

English

This dessert is crusty on top and juicy underneath; with a little yogurt on the side, it is perfect. In the winter months it can be made with canned fruit, such as apricots, pears, peaches, or cherries. The classic fresh fruit is apples in fall and apricots in summer. But try all the fruits and find your family favorites.

METHOD

· Preheat oven to 375° F (190° C).

> **Mind Refresher** ✿ Stand straight, breath normally;
> watch your breath for 30 seconds.

· Combine oats, flour, sugar, cinnamon, and salt in a medium
    mixing bowl.
· Mix in butter by rubbing between your fingertips to form a
    coarse meal.
· Arrange fruit in an 8 x 8 x 2–inch (20 x 20 x 5–cm) square
    baking dish.
· Pour in water and spread fruit with crumb mix, patting it down.
· Bake 1 hour or until top is brown and bubbly.

Serves 6–8

VARIATIONS

Apricots: You don't need as much apricot as you would other fruit. Use 10 apricots, sliced in fourths, and add ¼ cup (125 g) grated coconut to the topping.

Almonds or other nuts: Add to the topping mixture.

Pears: Use with freshly grated ginger and walnuts

Light and Creamy Custard

Spanish

This custard calls for more eggs than most, with extra soft results. Use high-quality ingredients, especially fresh eggs and milk. The caramelized sugar can be left out. The easiest way to serve this custard is to cool it at room temperature and scoop it directly from the pan. A true comfort food, it is an excellent dessert after any meal.

2 large eggs
6 egg yolks
¾ cup (175 g) granulated sugar
½ teaspoon vanilla extract
4 cups (1 L) whole milk

CARAMEL SAUCE
⅓ cup (90 g) granulated sugar
2 tablespoons water

METHOD

- Preheat oven to 350° F (180° C).
- Mix together all eggs and yolks, sugar, and vanilla in a mixing bowl until well blended.

> **Mind Refresher ✿** Stand straight, breathe normally, and concentrate on the in-and-out breath 3 times; as your mind wanders, bring it back to the breath.

- Heat milk in a medium saucepan over medium-high heat until hot.
- Pour hot milk slowly into egg mixture, stirring continuously.
- Make caramel sauce: Heat sugar and water in a small saucepan over medium heat, swirling pan frequently, until mixture begins to turn light nut color; watch carefully because it will turn very quickly.
- Pour caramel sauce immediately into an 8 x 8 x 2–inch (20 x 20 x 5–cm) baking pan, swirling it around to coat bottom. It is okay if the pan is not completely coated.
- Pour egg mixture through a strainer into baking pan.
- Place pan into a larger baking pan with 1-inch (2.5-cm) sides. Fill larger pan halfway with water to create water bath.
- Bake 1½ hours or until firm to the touch. Let cool at room temperature and serve, or refrigerate for a firmer custard.

Serves 6–8

VARIATION
Coconut custard with rum: Instead of 4 cups (1 L) milk, use 2 cups (500 ml) coconut milk and 2 cups (500 ml) milk, and use 1 tablespoon dark rum instead of vanilla extract.

butter for preparing pan
1 cup (150 g) all-purpose flour
8 tablespoons (4 ounces or 125 g)
   salted butter, divided:
   (5 tablespoons [75 g] and
   3 tablespoons [45 g]), cut into
   ½-inch (1.2-cm) cubes
pinch sea salt
¼ cup (60 ml) cold water
3–4 baking apples (1 pound)
⅓ cup (75 g) light brown sugar

Fall Apple Tart
French

An elegant French woman prepared this tart every Sunday for her husband because it was his favorite. The thin buttery crust is covered with apples in concentric circles. Nothing more—only the fresh flavor of apples. There is nothing better. The favorite apple in France is Reine des Reinettes or Belle de Boskoop. In America, Granny Smiths can be used. The crust can be made quickly in a food processor or by hand—the secret is to butter the tart pan. Served hot from the oven, this tart is sure to satisfy.

METHOD

- Preheat oven to 425° F (220° C).
- Butter a 9–10-inch (22.5-cm) tart pan.
- Combine flour and salt in a medium mixing bowl.
- Add 5 tablespoons (75 g) cubed butter to flour.
- Using your fingertips, work flour and butter together until mix resembles fine cornmeal.
- Add just enough water to gather all flour mix into a ball; sprinkle with flour to prevent sticking, cover, and set aside in refrigerator.
- Peel, halve, and core apples. Slice into ¼-inch (6-mm) slices.
- Place dough ball on lightly floured surface. Flatten with hand to make a thick circle. Flour both sides.
- Flour rolling pin. Roll dough from center in all directions to make a circle. Turn dough over; flour if it sticks; finish rolling to thin circle the size of tart pan.
- Fold dough in half and place in tart pan. Unfold dough and press around edges.
- Place apple slices around tart pan, beginning from the outside and ending in the middle. Overlap the apples to make a circular design.
- Sprinkle with sugar and dot with 3 tablespoons (45 g) butter.
- Bake in the middle rack of oven for 5 minutes. Reduce heat to 400° F (204° C) and continue baking 35–40 minutes or until golden brown and apples are tender.

Mind Refresher ✿ Serve with loving kindness.

Serves 6

MAKING BATTER IN FOOD PROCESSOR

Place flour, salt, and butter in food processor mixing bowl. Mix 2 seconds. Add water and mix until dough forms ball.

Motivation

Thus when I work for others' sake,
No reason can there be for boasting or amazement.
For it is just as when I feed myself—
I don't expect to be rewarded.

—SHANTIDEVA, seventh-century Indian poet and master
The Way of the Bodhisattva

CHAPTER 8

Snacks and Baking

for Hopes and Fears

Rock Star Carob Cookies

When I was first beginning to be a strict vegetarian, one day I tried baking without eggs, butter, and chocolate, instead using tofu, oil, and carob. I thought I would make the most delicious healthful cookies. Everyone would love them! I prepared them and couldn't wait to taste them. They smelled great as they were baking, but when I took my first bite, I found they were rock hard. Disappointed and discouraged, but not wanting to waste my efforts, I decided to serve the cookies as a midnight snack to a family of scavenging raccoons that nightly visited our back porch. I watched from my hiding place within the house as the father raccoon approached the dish. He flashed his teeth as he placed the cookie in his mouth. He could not chew. The cookie was too hard. Amazed, I watched him walk over to the cat's water bowl, dip the cookie, and begin chewing. The rest of the raccoon family followed his example of dipping and chewing. I vowed to be flexible like the raccoons. I revised the recipe and made the cookies for guests on several occasions; if they ever came out too hard, I called them "rock star carob cookies" and served them with a cup of tea for dipping.

— ROBIN EASTICK, *American*

Date-Sweetened Walnut Loaf

English

This excellent teacake, full of dates and topped with roasted walnuts, is often served thinly sliced at English tea tables. The English drink their tea all day long, even with their meals, and a cup of steaming hot tea with milk is often the first thing you are offered when you visit their homes. But there is nothing better than the formal tea hour, when you stop your day at four o'clock to enjoy a freshly brewed cup, delectable cakes and biscuits, and a visit with friends. This cake tastes wonderful toasted and served with butter or made with dried fruits such as prunes or raisins.

METHOD

· Preheat oven to 300° F (150° C).
· Lightly butter and dust with flour all sides of a 9 x 5 x 3–inch (23 x 13 x 6–cm) loaf pan.

Mind Refresher ✿ **Stand straight, relax, and breathe normally. As you chop the dates, think to yourself, "I am chopping the poisons of my mind, which contribute to my hopes and fears."**

· Chop dates with 2 tablespoons flour to make them easier to chop.
· In a medium mixing bowl, mix flour, salt, sugar, and ½ cup (75 g) walnuts.
· Mix in egg and butter with dates. Stir into flour mixture until batter is soft and sticky.
· Pour batter into loaf pan. Sprinkle remaining nuts on top.
· Bake, uncovered, 2 hours or until brown and a knife inserted comes out clean.
· Let cool in pan.
· Take cake out of pan and store in a tightly fitted container or wrap with plastic wrap. This loaf gets better the next day.
· Slice thinly and enjoy with a cup of tea.

Serves 8

butter and flour for preparing pan
1 pound (500 g) dates, pitted
2 tablespoons all-purpose flour
1 teaspoon baking soda
1 cup (250 ml) boiling-hot water
2 cups (300 g) all-purpose flour
¼ teaspoon sea salt
⅓ cup (75 g) light brown or raw sugar
1 cup (150 g) chopped walnuts, divided
1 large egg, beaten
3 tablespoons (45 g) unsalted butter, melted

butter for preparing pan

2 cups (16 ounces or 500 g) golden sweet cream-style corn

1 cup (175 g) yellow cornmeal

¾ cup (175 g) milk

¼ cup (60 ml) vegetable oil

1 large egg, beaten

¼ teaspoon baking powder

¼ teaspoon sea salt

1 (7-ounce or 200-g) can whole green chilies, drained and sliced into strips, or about 6 fresh poblano or Anaheim chilies, peeled

1 cup (125 g) shredded Mexican melting cheese (Monterey Jack or mild cheddar)

Mexican Corn Bread

North American, from Sedona, Arizona

This cornbread was the first dish my friend's mother made for her father after they were married, and it became a family favorite for potlucks. Not a dry cornbread, it has a moist, rich consistency, full of cheese and chilies. In a typical southwestern meal, it would be found alongside steak and beans. It can also be served as a casserole with a big green salad. Cut it into squares and serve it at the table right from the baking pan.

METHOD

· Preheat oven to 350° F (180° C).

· Butter an 8 x 8 x 2–inch (20 x 20 x 5–cm) baking pan.

> **Mind Refresher** ✿ Stand straight, breathe normally, and concentrate on the breath's in-and-out movement as you mix the batter.

· In a medium mixing bowl, mix creamed corn, cornmeal, milk, oil, eggs, baking powder, and salt until well blended.

· Pour ⅓ batter into baking pan. Sprinkle with ⅓ chilies and ⅓ cheese. Repeat twice with remaining chilies and cheese.

· Bake 45 minutes–1 hour or until brown and firm to the touch.

· Cool 30 minutes before serving.

Serves 6–8

Auntie Rena Brown Bread

German, from Berlin

After trying this recipe, you won't be able to say you can't make bread—this one is so simple to make. The trick is to bake it in a non-preheated oven. German breads are heavy but absolutely delicious. The woman who gave the recipe to me got it from her aunt, who would always buy whole wheat and whole barley and then mill her own flour, experimenting to find the texture she liked. The bread is very nutritious and tastes better a day or two after it is made. It will last a long time. Germans keep their bread in wood, metal, or porcelain containers or on a wooden board outside. In the mornings they eat it with jam, served with an egg and coffee or tea. Lunch is their hot meal, but at dinnertime they use the bread for sandwiches, served with soup or salad.

vegetable oil for preparing pan

2 cups (500 ml) cold water

1 cup (125 g) quick-cooking oats

½ cup (125 g) Quark, fromage blanc, sour cream, or Greek-style yogurt

1 tablespoon sea salt

1 teaspoon herb salt

½ cup (75 g) sunflower seeds

1 cup (150 g) flax or sesame seeds

1 package (¼ ounce or 7.5 g) rapid-rise yeast powder or 1 tablespoon baking powder

2½ cups (375 g) whole-wheat flour

½ cup (75 g) barley flour

2 tablespoons sunflower seeds

METHOD

· Grease a 9 x 5 x 3–inch (23 x 13 x 6–cm) loaf pan with oil.
· In a large mixing bowl, combine water, oatmeal, cream, salt, herb salt, sunflower seeds, flax or sesame seeds, and yeast.

Mind Refresher ✿ Stand straight, breathe normally, and watch the breath for 30 seconds. Beat out aggression as you mix in the flour.

· Mix in flour, vigorously, by hand or with an electric mixer, until well mixed.
· Pour batter into loaf pan.
· Sprinkle top with sunflower seeds.
· Bake in non-preheated 475° F (240° C) oven on the bottom shelf 1 hour or until brown and firm.
· Remove pan from oven and let cool.
· Remove bread from pan and store 1 day before slicing.

Serves 8

VARIATION

Use unbleached flour and cornmeal instead of whole-wheat and barley flour.

2 cups (300 g) all-purpose flour
1 teaspoon baking soda
1 teaspoon sea salt
4 tablespoons (60 g) butter, cut
    into ½-inch (1.2-cm) cubes
½ cup (80 g) raisins
¼ cup (30 g) finely chopped
    candied orange peel
1 tablespoon granulated sugar
¾ cup (75 ml) buttermilk
flour for dusting surfaces

Orange and Raisin Soda Bread

Irish

A soda bread is a floury round loaf with a crisscross pattern on top; it is traditionally made in a mold and cooked in a wood-burning stove. This one is flavored with raisins and candied orange peel. Ireland has many varieties of soda bread—wheaten bread, made with three quarters whole-wheat flour and one quarter white flour, and treacle bread, made with molasses—are just a couple of examples. Serve this bread with a good cup of Irish black tea and whole milk.

METHOD

· Preheat oven to 450° F (230° C).
· Combine flour, baking soda, and salt in a medium mixing bowl.

Mind Refresher ✿ Stand straight, breathe normally, and concentrate on your hands as you rub butter into flour.

· Rub butter cubes into flour mixture, between your fingertips, to a coarse, cornmeal-like texture.
· Stir in raisins, candied peel, and sugar.
· Make a well in the center and stir in enough buttermilk to make a soft dough that holds together.
· Turn onto a well-floured surface and form into a 7-inch (17.5-cm) round, 1 inch (2.5 cm) thick.
· Lightly dust an ungreased baking sheet with flour.
· Place dough on baking sheet. Using a knife, cut one large crisscross, ½ inch (1.2 cm) deep, on top.
· Bake 30–35 minutes or until brown and firm.

Serves 6–8

Crisp and Chewy Cookies

North American

I created this classic chocolate chip cookie recipe in France for French tastes. The cookies are not too sweet, soft in the center, and crispy at the edges. The recipe can be altered to suit various preferences. The classic version is made with butter, but you can use oil if you add a cup of oats to the batter. To make crisp cookies—that is, crisp and brown around the edges and soft in the middle—bake them twelve to fifteen minutes; soft cookies take about ten minutes. The secret to getting a light, crisp cookie is to beat the butter and sugar well. Cookie size can vary from one to four inches. Enjoy them with a cappuccino.

1 cup (250 g) unsalted butter, softened
1¼ cups (260 g) light brown or raw sugar
1 teaspoon vanilla extract
2 large eggs
2¼ cups (325 g) all-purpose flour
1 teaspoon sea salt
1 teaspoon baking soda
1½ cups (300 g) semisweet chocolate chips or 3 semisweet chocolate bars, coarsely chopped
1 cup (150 g) chopped walnuts

METHOD

· Preheat oven to 375° F (190° C).
· Beat butter, sugar, and vanilla in a large mixing bowl until smooth and light lemon in color.
· Beat eggs into butter mixture until light and fluffy.
· Mix together flour, salt, and baking soda in a small mixing bowl.
· Stir flour mixture gradually into butter until well blended.
· If desired, divide dough into 3 parts (about 1 cup or 250 g each) to make different types of cookies; otherwise, use all of it for chocolate chip cookies.

> **Mind Refresher** ✿ Stand straight, breathe normally, and taste one chocolate chip. Concentrate on the taste in your mouth; as the mind wanders and labels, return to the taste sensation.

· Stir chocolate chips and nuts or other cookie ingredients into dough.
· Drop by rounded teaspoon onto ungreased baking sheets.
· Bake on upper shelf of oven 10–15 minutes or until golden brown, crisp around edges, and almost firm in the center. Let stand a few minutes and then place cookies on wire racks to cool. Store in airtight containers.

Makes about 4 dozen 2-inch (5-cm) cookies (about 3 cups [750 g] of dough)

VARIATIONS FOR 1 CUP OF DOUGH

Chocolate mocha: Add 1 tablespoon unsweetened cocoa powder, 1 teaspoon strong coffee, ⅔ cup (175 g) plain or white chocolate chips, and ⅓ cup (45 g) chopped walnuts.

Dried fruit: Add ⅔ cup (175 g) chopped dates or dried fruit, ⅓ cup (45 g) chopped nuts, and ⅓ cup (45 g) shredded coconut.

Sushi Balls to Go

Japanese

The Japanese take sushi balls along when traveling because they provide good steady energy. Umeboshi plums are pinkish red and salt-pickled, with a sour salty taste. They aid digestion, enhance the immune system, and are very alkaline. They can be found in Japanese markets or natural food stores.

1 cup (250 g) freshly cooked
   short-grain rice
6 umeboshi plums, pitted
2 nori seaweed sheets
toasted sesame oil

METHOD

Mind Refresher ✿ Stand straight, breathe normally, and watch the movement of your mind for 30 seconds.

· Wet hands and press some cooked rice into a small ball. Make a hole in the center, place inside an umeboshi plum, and press rice to re-form ball. Repeat this procedure with remaining rice and plums.
· Put balls in a tight-fitting container.
· Cut nori seaweed sheets into thirds.
· Brush squares with sesame oil and lightly toast over flame.
· Put toasted sheets in container with rice balls, cover, and take on your trip.
· At snack time, roll together nori squares and rice balls.

Makes 6

1 cup (225 g) granulated sugar
⅓ cup (75 ml) milk
1 teaspoon ground cinnamon
1 teaspoon sea salt
1 teaspoon vanilla extract
2½ cups (250 g) walnut halves

Candied Cinnamon Walnuts

German

These make excellent Christmas gifts wrapped in pretty bundles. People are always wanting more and look forward to receiving them each year. Keep them on hand for adding to salads with sliced apples and blue cheese. The German woman who gave me this recipe serves them with beer.

METHOD

- Combine sugar, milk, cinnamon, and salt in a large saucepan. Cook over high heat, stirring, until sugar dissolves.
- Boil to softball stage, 234° F (190° C) on a candy thermometer, or until a small amount dropped into very cold water forms a soft ball that flattens when removed from water.
- Remove from heat and stir in vanilla.
- Stir in walnuts until coated and creamy.
- Turn out onto aluminum foil. Leave to cool until sugar coating is firm.

Mind Refresher ✿ Stand straight, breathe normally, and taste a walnut; as the mind wonders, return to the taste sensation.

- Break apart walnuts that are stuck together and store in a tight-fitting container.

Makes about 2½ cups (750 g)

2½ cups (375 g) all-purpose flour
1 tablespoon whole-wheat flour
¼ teaspoon sea salt
2 teaspoons ghee or vegetable oil
½–¾ cup (125–175 ml) warm
  water
1–2 tablespoons (30 g) ghee or
  butter, melted

Chapatis

Indian, from Dehra Dun

In Indian households, chapatis are placed on the table daily, with each meal. These unyeasted flat breads are very similar to Mexican flour tortillas. They are made out of a finely milled soft whole-wheat flour called *ata*, which can be found at Indian markets. In one Indian family's kitchen, the mother would make the dough in a mixing bowl, kneading it effortlessly and dividing it into balls. The dough balls would sit until serving time, when she would roll them out to thin rounds on a wooden slab and fry them in a cast-iron skillet. The chapatis were put in a covered container and brought to the table. They were delicious. For less fuss, you may purchase them ready-made in many grocery and natural food stores. Fresh chapatis can be stored for three to four days in a tight-fitting container or frozen for a couple of months.

METHOD

· Mix flours, salt, and ½ teaspoon ghee in a medium mixing bowl.
· Gradually pour in water, working mixture with your hand to form
    a ball.

> **Mind Refresher** ✿ Stand straight, breathe normally,
> and focus on your breath for 30 seconds.
> Now knead with awareness.

· On a floured surface, knead dough by folding and pressing 5 minutes,
    until it is silky smooth, or mix it in a food processor for 5 minutes.
    Add flour and water as necessary. Test dough by pushing finger
    into it; if the hole stays, dough is ready.
· Cover well and set aside 1 hour at room temperature.
· Knead dough briefly and divide into 12 balls; keep balls covered.
· On a floured suface, press each ball into a patty and roll into a thin
    8-inch (20-cm) circle; keep covered until ready to fry.
· Heat medium skillet over high heat until hot.
· Slap 1 chapati onto hot skillet; cook until light brown spots appear
    underneath. Turn over and cook other side until light brown spots
    appear.
· Put in a covered container or wrap in clean cloth until serving time.
· At serving time, pass each over a hot flame—do this on both sides very
    quickly. They will swell, fill with steam, and have black spots.
· Stack in a serving container, dribbling each with ghee, cover, and
    serve.

Makes 12 8-inch (20-cm) chapatis

Apple Cake of My Mama

Ukrainian

This moist cake, chock-full of apples, is easy to prepare and has no butter. The buttery taste comes from the apples and eggs. In Ukraine, it is served as an after-school snack and at teas, birthdays, and other parties. With the caramel butter frosting, it is a rich cake, but it can also be prepared with just a dusting of confectioners' sugar, instant cocoa, and chopped walnuts on top. The easiest way to prepare it is not to frost and to serve directly from the pan.

METHOD

- Preheat oven to 450° F (230° C).
- Butter an 8 x 8 x 2–inch (20 x 20 x 5–cm) square baking pan.

> **Mind Refresher ✿** Stand straight, breathe normally, and watch your mind for 30 seconds. Prepare the cake while being aware of the mind's expectation of how it will turn out.

- In a medium mixing bowl, beat eggs with sugar and vanilla until smooth and light lemon in color.
- Stir in flour and baking powder; mix until smooth.
- Arrange apples at the bottom of baking pan.
- Pour batter over apples, moving with spoon to distribute into apples.
- Reduce oven temperature to 325° F (160° C) and bake cake 35–40 minutes or until brown and firm to the touch. Remove from oven and let cool to frost, or eat warm out of pan without frosting.
- Take cake out of baking pan by inverting it onto a plate; then invert it again onto a serving plate.
- Frost cake with caramel butter glaze and sprinkle with cocoa powder and walnuts. Or just sprinkle with confectioners' sugar, cocoa powder, and walnuts.

Serves 6–8

butter for preparing the pan
4 large eggs
1 cup (225 g) granulated sugar
1 teaspoon vanilla extract
1 cup (150 g) all-purpose flour
1½ teaspoons baking powder
5–6 green apples (1½ pounds or 750 g), peeled and cut into ½-inch (1.2-cm) pieces (about 5 cups)

TOPPING
caramel butter glaze (see "Frostings," below) or dusting of confectioners' sugar and cocoa powder
¾ cup (75 g) chopped walnuts

FROSTINGS
Caramel butter glaze: Melt 6 tablespoons butter in a small saucepan and cook until lightly brown; remove from heat and stir in ⅔ cup (125 g) confectioners' sugar, 1 teaspoon vanilla extract, and ¼ cup (60 ml) cold water until smooth. Cool to set for frosting.

1 cup (8 ounces or 250 ml) milk
   or soymilk
1 tablespoon jam (forest berry,
   raspberry, or strawberry)

Jam Milk

Swedish

In Sweden, the forests are rich with wild berries—cranberries, blueberries, cloudberries, and raspberries. So it is very common for people to have cupboards full of beautiful jams, with colors ranging from golds to reds. This snack, called "poor man's dessert" in Sweden, is simply jam mixed with milk. It is an easy after-school treat for kids.

METHOD

· Pour milk into glass.
· Stir in jam until mixed.
· Drink with a straw.

> **Mind Refresher** ❂ Appreciate whatever is happening.

Makes an 8-ounce (250-ml) glass

3 cups (400 g) all-purpose flour
3 cups (720 ml) water
6 tablespoons cream of tartar
3 tablespoons vegetable oil
1½ cups (500 g) sea salt
food coloring (red, orange, blue,
   yellow)
essential oils (lavender, orange,
   or other)

Essential Oil Playdough

North American

This "recipe" makes for lots of fun. Let the kids use kitchen utensils—cookie cutters, spoons, rolling pins, and jar tops—to play with this dough. The essential oils add that extra something. Choose the smells you like. No eating—it tastes terrible!

METHOD

· Combine all ingredients in a large saucepan over medium heat until they stick together, forming a mass.
· Remove from heat and divide dough into different parts.

> **Mind Refresher** ❂ Focus on the colors, textures, and aromas as you work the dough.

· Add magic colors and drops of essential oil. Work dough with hands until color and oil are well blended.
· Store in covered containers.

Makes 4 cups (1 kg)

1 tablespoon vegetable oil or
  olive oil
½ cup (125 g) popcorn
½ cup (60 g) nutritional yeast
1–2 tablespoons tamari or Bragg
  Liquid Aminos
¼ teaspoon ground cayenne
grated Parmesan or other cheese
  (optional)
sea salt

Aloha Theater Seasoned Popcorn
Hawaiian

This popcorn was served at the Aloha Theater in Kona, Hawaii. It was great to be able to go to the movies and get a big bag of popcorn that left you feeling good. It's a perfect snack when you want something a little nutty, salty, spicy, and crisp. The nutritional yeast creates the nutty flavor, the tamari adds the salt, and the cayenne provides the spice. Yum! Note: Popcorn pops better when the corns are stored in the refrigerator.

METHOD

· Heat oil in a large heavy pot over medium-high heat until hot.
· Pour in popcorn and cover pot.

> **Mind Refresher** ✿ As corn pops, wish that
> all minds may be popped open and filled
> with wisdom and compassion.

· As corn starts to pop, shake pan until all corn is popped.
· Pour into serving bowl and toss with yeast, tamari, cayenne, and
  cheese.
· Season to taste with salt.

Makes 8 cups or 1 large bowl

VARIATIONS
Toss with melted butter and sea salt.
Toss with fresh lime juice and ground cayenne.
Toss with melted butter and granulated sugar.
Toss with olive oil, Bragg Liquid Aminos, gomashio (see page 124),
garlic powder, and ground cayenne.

Finer Than Flour

One's view should be as high, deep, and vast as the sky, whereas one's attention to actions and their effects should be as subtle and fine as refined flour.

—PADMASAMBHAVA,
great tantric master in Tibet,
also known as Guru Rinpoche

Views

It is said that if we take one thing to be the truth and cling to it, even if truth itself comes in person and knocks at our door, we won't open it. For things to reveal themselves to us, we need to be ready to abandon our views about them.

—BUDDHA SHAKYAMUNI,
universal Buddha who lived
about 2,500 years ago

CHAPTER 9

Drinks and
Remedies

for Impermanence

The Tea Cup

An arrogant Japanese professor went to visit a master in Japan to inquire about Zen. The master offered him tea. Placing the cup down, he poured until the cup was full to the brim. The professor watched in amazement as the master continued to pour and the tea overflowed all over the table. The professor could no longer contain himself. "The cup is full! No more will go in!" he screamed. "Like this cup," said the master calmly, "you are overflowing with your opinions and concepts. How can I show you Zen unless you first empty your cup?"

— **UNKNOWN,** *Japanese*

Maté

Argentinean

yerba maté tea leaves
hot (but not boiling) water

In Argentina, friends call each other and say, "Let's get together and have a maté." The social equivalent of coffee in the United States, maté is the Argentinean national drink. A member of the holly family, yerba maté (*Ilex paraguariensis*) is an evergreen tree that reaches up to twenty-six feet, with leaves that are somewhat leathery. It grows near streams in the wild. More stimulating than coffee or tea and very rich in minerals and vitamins, the plant is used throughout South America as a caffeine substitute, to sharpen mental alertness, to improve digestion, as a stimulant, and as an overall tonic. Research supports these medicinal benefits.

You need two objects to drink maté like an Argentinean: a *bombella*, which is a kind of straw made of stainless steel, and a small gourd, about seven inches in height. The drink is made in the gourd and then passed around the table and refilled as it is emptied. Use hot but not boiling water—boiling-hot water burns the leaves. The process can be repeated as long as you like the taste, which becomes increasingly weak with each steeping. When you are finished, throw out the leaves and wash the gourd with water only, not soap. Of course, if you are in a hurry, you can make maté from tea bags or from loose leaves steeped in a teapot.

METHOD

- Fill a gourd or a small pitcher two-thirds full with maté leaves. Move leaves to the side.
- Pour just enough water into empty side to avoid moistening top of leaves. Let sit a few minutes to swell leaves.
- Put *bombella* in side with water and then fill gourd three-quarters full with hot water.
- Let sit a minute without stirring.

> **Mind Refresher** ✿ Before drinking the tea, sit straight and hold the gourd between your hands, feeling its heat. Concentrate on this sensation for 30 seconds.

- Suck the drink through the straw.
- Share the maté with friends by passing it around the table.
- When gourd is empty, cover same leaves with more hot water.

SUGGESTIONS

Seasoning the gourd for first-time use: Fill gourd half full of leaves. Wet with enough water to swell the leaves. As they dry out, keep rewetting the leaves for three days. Then toss out the leaves and rinse the gourd with water.

Different maté flavors: Add lemon peel, orange peel, fresh mint, or licorice root.

½ cup (125 g) fruit, fresh or
  frozen, roughly chopped (frozen
  fruit makes for a thicker shake)
½–1 banana, fresh or frozen,
  roughly chopped
1 cup (250 ml) juice, low-fat milk,
  yogurt, or soymilk
1 tablespoon nuts or seeds
  (optional)
1 tablespoon dried fruit, raisins,
  dates, or crystallized ginger
  (optional)
1–2 tablespoons spirulina powder,
  bee pollen, or protein powder
  (optional)
pinch cinnamon, ginger, or nutmeg

Blender Smoothie

North American, from California

Smoothies are good for starting the day or for an afternoon pick-me-up. The banana with apple or orange flavor combination works well; add dates and raisins for extra sweetness. Spirulina, a dried blue-green micro-algae, provides a source of protein, B vitamins, and vitamin A. Its high chlorophyll content makes it very green, and though it has no flavor, many people are turned off by the color. Bee pollen is sometimes added to increase energy and stamina, but use caution at first because some people are allergic to it. High-quality protein powder can be found in natural food stores. For the nuts and seeds, try flaxseeds (rich in essential fatty acids), sunflower seeds, or almonds. Add powdered cinnamon, ginger, or nutmeg to keep the digestive fire warm. Create your own favorite smoothie flavor combination.

METHOD

Mind Refresher ✿ Stand straight, breathe normally,
and blend ingredients with the motivation to
blend all mind's poisons, transforming them
into love and wisdom.

· Put all ingredients into an electric blender and blend to desired
  consistency.
· Pour into a glass and drink.

Makes 1½ cups (350 ml)

A Cup of Tea

Asian

3 cups (720 ml) water (2 cups
  [500 ml] and 1 cup [250 ml])
2 teaspoons Darjeeling tea leaves

This recipe for the perfect cup of Darjeeling tea is for when you have all the time in the world, as in a Jane Austen novel. Darjeeling tea comes from the Himalayas around Mount Kanchenjungha, where on a clear day Mount Everest is visible in the distance. The first flush, grown in May and June, is light and exquisitely flavored. The second flush, produced in June and July, is exceptional, often with a muscatel-like bouquet. After July, both the quality and the price of Darjeeling decrease. The rule of thumb in making a pot of tea is to use one teaspoon per person, plus one "for the pot."

METHOD

> **Mind Refresher** ✿ Stand straight, relax, and breathe normally. While making the tea, use patience as your object of focus.

- Fill a small saucepan with 2 cups (500 ml) water, cover, place tea leaves on lid, and bring water to a boil over high heat. This method warms the tea leaves and releases their flavor.
- Set aside tea leaves. Fill teapot with hot water and set aside.
- Heat 1 cup (250 ml) water in saucepan until just beginning to boil. You don't want to under- or over-boil water.
- Pour out water in teapot. Add heated tea leaves.
- Pour barely boiled water over tea leaves.
- Cover and steep 3–5 minutes.
- Serve with milk and sugar, if desired.

Makes 1 cup (250 ml)

2½ cups (600 ml) water

1 rounded tablespoon or 1 handful
   of herbs

Herbal Infusions

Universal

Herbal teas (tisanes) make nice alternatives to black and green teas. Not only are they enjoyable to drink, but they also have medicinal properties. Their tastes cover all the flavor bases—bitter, sweet, spicy, sour, and salty—and they can be cooling or warming to the system; those are some of the qualities one would consider when making a formula for therapeutic purposes. While the medicinal uses of herbal teas are beyond the scope of this book, by choosing to drink herbal teas for pleasure you will also be giving your body the benefits of those herbs. It's fun to grow your own, drying them and storing them in brown paper bags to have available for teas throughout the year. They can also be used to flavor black or green tea. Try mint, nettles, comfrey, lemon balm, anise, sage, or rose.

METHOD

· Warm a teapot by filling it with hot water and letting it stand.
· Bring 2½ cups (600 ml) water to a boil over high heat.
· Discard water from teapot and place herbs inside.
· Pour boiling water into teapot.
· Let stand before serving. Steeping time varies according to particular herbal mix. For most mixes, try 10 minutes; next time increase or decrease to your tastes. Mint takes 5 minutes.

Mind Refresher ✿ Serve with the motivation to bring others happiness.

Makes 2 cups (500 ml)

VARIATIONS

Teas with roots and seeds: Put roots and seeds in a small saucepan with water, bring to a boil, pour into the teapot, and steep 15 minutes.

HERBAL FLAVOR OPTIONS

- Lemony: Lemon verbena, lemon and orange peels, lemongrass, lemon thyme, lemon balm
- Sweet: Anise, fennel, licorice, stevia, vanilla bean, hyssop
- Tart: Rosehips, hibiscus
- Woodsy: Sassafras, sarsaparilla, burdock
- Floral: Flowers of blue malva, chamomile, lavender, rose, calendula
- Fresh: Peppermint, spearmint
- Aromatic: Sage, rosemary, verbena

FAVORITE FRENCH ONE-HERB TISANES

- Thyme
- Verbena *(verveine)*
- Cassis leaves (black currant)
- Mint *(menthe)*
- Burdock
- Linden *(tilleul)*

TWO-HERB TEA BLENDS

- Thyme and a little hyssop
- Rosemary and lavender
- Clove and a little chamomile
- Marjoram and mint
- Chamomile and hibiscus flowers
- Elderflower and peppermint
- Nettles with mint
- Lemon balm and lavender
- Rosemary and hibiscus flowers
- Sage with lemon verbena
- Yarrow and peppermint
- Basil and lemon verbena

THREE-HERB TEA BLENDS

- Cassis, yarrow, and elderflower
- Marjoram, angelica, and lavender
- Yarrow, rosemary, and hyssop
- Thyme, sage, and rosemary
- Serpolet thyme, lavender, and marjoram
- Angelica, lemon thyme, and marjoram

2 tablespoons or 1 handful dried
    nettle leaves
2 cups (500 ml) water

Green Nettle Tea

European

Everyone talks about "eating your greens." Stinging nettles, *Urtica dioica*, is a wild herb available to everyone, often right out your back door. It is easy to collect your own or to find dried in natural food stores. Milarepa, Tibet's great yogi, lived on nettles, which he found outside his cave. This fantastic plant is a great friend, especially to women. She has the ability to nourish our overall well-being; strengthen and rebuild kidneys and adrenals; ease cystitis and bloating; stabilize blood sugar; reduce fatigue and exhaustion; support the immune system; and nourish the digestive, nervous, and endocrine systems. She is also very good for pregnant women because of her blood-building qualities. When you feel a cold coming, a cup of nettle tea works wonders because nettles are high in vitamin C. Indeed, they are full of vitamins, minerals, proteins, and micronutrients that can nourish every bit of you.

In nature, nettle plants stand tall with a beautiful green color, looking like giant mint plants. They do sting, so wear your gloves. Pick the branches in spring and early summer, before the flowers emerge. Store fresh nettles on paper in a dark room or hang them in bundles to dry. Then remove the leaves from the stems and store them in brown paper bags. Fresh nettles are good for the compost heap, in soups, and juiced (to use them for juicing, place the leaves in ice-cube trays with water and freeze; take out a cube and melt it when you're ready to juice). The French and Tibetans eat nettles as a soup, while the English like to mix them with their black tea.

METHOD

· Put nettle leaves and water in a saucepan and bring to a boil; simmer 10 minutes.
· Turn off heat, cover, and let sit 10 minutes.

> **Mind Refresher ✿** Reflect on impermanence,
> how everything is changing.

· Drink one or more cups a day.

Makes 2 cups (500 ml)

SUGGESTION

Make the nettle tea right before bed and let it steep in a covered jar overnight. The longer it sits, the greener it will be.

Roasted-Twig Bancha Tea

Japanese

8 cups (2 L) cold water
⅓ cup (22 g) bancha tea twigs

Cha means "tea" in Japanese. This neutral green tea is made from the leaves and twigs of a Japanese bush. Unlike many teas, bancha is mildly alkaline and high in citric acid. It can be found in tea bags or in bulk. The following recipe makes enough tea to fill a thermos to drink from throughout the day. To make one cup, follow this method using one teaspoon of tea and one and a half cups of water and cooking over low heat for five minutes.

METHOD

· Put water and tea in a medium saucepan and bring to a boil over high heat; reduce heat to low and cook 10 minutes.
· Strain tea into a thermos.

> **Mind Refresher** ✿ Pour yourself a cup of tea. Sit down, hold the hot teacup between the palms of your hands, and enjoy your tea.

Makes 8 cups (2 L)

HEALTHFUL VARIATIONS

For an overall tonic effect: Put in a drinking cup 1 teaspoon kudzu powder, ⅙ umeboshi plum, and ½ teaspoon ginger juice or grated ginger. Add a little cold water to prevent lumping, stir to dissolve kudzu powder, and then add hot bancha tea and drink. Kudzu is a white starch made from the root of the wild kudzu plant. It is an alkaline-forming food, useful for strengthening the intestines. Umeboshi plums are pickled in sea salt and shiso (beefsteak plant); they are highly alkaline, aid in digestion, and promote healthy intestinal flora. Ginger juice is also alkaline-forming; to make it, grate ginger root and squeeze the pulp through a cheesecloth.

For colds or low energy: Add ½ teaspoon tamari to 1 cup (250 ml) hot bancha tea and drink. Do this 3 times a day.

Red Hibiscus Apple Cooler

North American, from California

1 ounce (30 g) red clover
3 ounces (90 g) hibiscus flowers
⅓ ounce (15 g) cinnamon sticks,
    broken up
6 whole cloves
4 cups (1 L) water
1 cup (250 ml) apple juice
1 teaspoon honey
apple or orange slices (optional)

This delicious cooler blends herbal tea and fruit juice and is very thirst-quenching in warmer weather. With its bright flavors and red color, it is great as a party punch, with fruit or flowers mixed in. The spices aid digestion, so the coolness of the fruit doesn't weaken the digestive fire. They can be found in natural food stores or ordered online. Store unused spice blend in a jar for future use.

METHOD

· Mix red clover, hibiscus flowers, cinnamon sticks, and cloves
    together in a medium bowl.

Mind Refresher ❂ Stand straight, breathe normally, and
    concentrate on the aroma of the spices for 30 seconds.

· In a saucepan, bring 4 cups (1 L) water to a boil over high heat.
· Turn off heat, stir in 1 ounce (30 g) herbal blend, cover, and steep
    20 minutes.
· Strain and then stir in apple juice and honey. Refrigerate.
· Garnish with fruit slices just before serving,

Makes 1 quart (1 L)

PARTY-SIZE COOLER

Bring 1 gallon (4 L) of water to a boil; turn off heat, add 3 ounces (90 g) hibiscus cooler herbal blend, and steep 20 minutes. Strain and then stir in 1 quart (1 L) apple juice and 1 tablespoon honey. Refrigerate. Garnish with fruit slices just before serving.

Herb Farm Tisane Remedies

French, from Brittany

In the French countryside, people drink herbal teas, or tisanes, for common ailments. The following blends can be made to have on hand for problems with digestion, sleep, milk flow for new mothers, and bronchitis. The herb farm where these recipes come from was the great place to go for a cup of herbal tea. The kitchen was warm and cozy, with a large wooden table and six dogs and six cats. When the proprietor was not serving tea in her home, she sold her fresh herbs at local markets. The herbs can be found in natural food stores or ordered online.

FOR DIGESTION (GAS) AND MILK FLOW

Drink this tea after meals for gas. Women with babies should drink 2 cups (500 ml) a day during their lactation. Prepare a blend of equal parts caraway, fennel, anise, coriander, and dill seed. To make the tea, use 1 tablespoon seeds per 2 cups (500 ml) water. Put seeds in water, bring to a boil, cover, and steep 15 minutes.

FOR STRESS AND SLEEP

If you are feeling stressed or are having trouble sleeping through the night, this is a good tea to drink 30 minutes before going to bed. Blend 2 parts dried California poppy, 1 part dried marjoram, and 1 part dried lavender. Use 1 tablespoon herbs per 1 cup (250 ml) boiling water. Let steep 10 minutes.

FOR BRONCHITIS

Drink this tisane throughout the day when you have a chest cold. Blend equal parts dried hyssop, dried serpolet (wild thyme), and dried lavender, marjoram, or oregano. Use 1 tablespoon herbs per 2 cups (500 ml) boiling water. Let steep 10 minutes.

Mind Refresher ✿ Before drinking, hold the cup of tisane and enjoy the aroma of the herbs and the warmth of the cup.

Sangria

Spanish

Sangria is a festive Spanish drink made with red wine and fruit that has marinated overnight. In Spain it is served with tapas or before a paella meal. For a refreshing summer cooler, this drink can be made with white wine. Add different fruits in season, such as peaches, strawberries, kiwis, and apples, with mint leaves as a final touch.

4 cups (1 L) dry red wine
¼–½ cup (55–112 g) sugar or
   to taste
1 orange, with rind, sliced
1 lemon, with rind, sliced
¼ cup (60 ml) vodka (optional)
2 cups (500 ml) carbonated water
ice cubes

METHOD

Mind Refresher ❂ Stand straight, breathe normally, and watch your mind as distractions arise.

- Mix together wine, sugar, orange slices, lemon slices, and vodka in a large mixing bowl.
- Cover bowl and refrigerate overnight.
- Stir in carbonated water and ice cubes. Serve in tall glasses with fruit.

Serves 6–8

Having Overdone It, How to Undo It!

IF YOU'VE EATEN TOO MUCH:	UNDO IT BY TAKING:
fats	lemon tea, radishes
meat, eggs, cheese	vegetable juices, vegetable soup, fruits, salads
sugar	bancha tea with tamari, miso soup
sweets and flour products	vegetable soups, green vegetables, juices
fruits, salads, and raw food	warming seasonings, cooked food

The Chinese Approach to Keeping the Body in Balance

The Chinese have long known that the nature of food is more subtle than its measurable components—proteins, carbohydrates, fats, vitamins, and minerals. In considering a particular food, they note its energetic properties (cooling, neutral, or warming), its flavors (sour, bitter, sweet, pungent/spicy, salty), the season, appropriate cooking methods, and complementary herbs. Understanding a few of the culinary principles they employ can greatly help us to build stronger immune systems and increase our energy levels.

A key concept in Chinese nutrition is digestive fire. Most foods and cooking methods are said to either increase or decrease digestive fire (some foods and cooking methods have a neutral effect). For instance, ingredients such as ginger, garlic, and onions, and cooking methods, such as stir-frying and slow-cooking, increase digestive fire. Thus these ingredients and methods are used more during the colder months, when our digestive fire is naturally cooler. Cayenne, black pepper, and chilies are also used in tiny amounts to drive away cold from the body. Conversely, in spring and summer, when the weather is warmer, more neutral-to-cooling foods and cooking methods are used to keep the internal temperature cooler.

Digestive fire is compared to a flame under a pot of soup—if the flame goes out, the soup won't cook. The goal in Chinese nutrition is to create a balanced system, neither too cool nor too warm. That said, extreme cold is particularly to be avoided; ice-cold food like ice-cream, drinks with ice, and food right out of the fridge simply put out digestive fire. So instead of ice water, the Chinese drink hot water with meals. By heating food and beverages, regardless of their inherent properties, one is applying some warming quality to them. The idea is to keep the digestive fire warm enough to properly digest food.

With this basic concept in mind, we can begin to see how eating a lot of salads and other uncooked foods all year long might make us feel cold, bloated, lethargic, and gassy after a while. Eating raw foods might be helpful for a short period, to help cool an overheated system, but if your system is already on the cooler side, these foods will just cool the digestive fire even further, creating digestive problems.

A cool system needs neutral-to-warming energies to help with digestion. On the other hand, overheated types should not indulge in too much hot, spicy food. Younger adults and children tend to be more heated, while older people tend to be more cooled. As noted already, seasons also influence our internal temperatures, as does climate. In other words, whether your system is too cool, too hot, or just right varies with time and circumstances. Many of us have both tendencies, so in general it's a good idea to use neutral foods and cooking methods and to blend cooling and warming foods.

In this day and age, everything is available in the supermarket year-round, and you can find whatever you desire whenever you desire it. But eating in this way is not always best for your health. When considering what to buy and eat, bear in mind that fresh, local, and seasonal foods tend to be the ones whose energetic properties and flavors are most balancing.

ENERGETIC PROPERTIES OF SOME FOODS

Cooling: avocado, button mushrooms, celery, cucumbers, eggplant, green peppers, lettuce, radishes, seaweed, spinach, summer squash, tomatoes; mung beans, kidney beans, miso, tofu; apples, cantaloupe, bananas, lemons, oranges, pears, watermelon; milk, yogurt; millet, barley, buckwheat, wheat.

Neutral: beets, broccoli, cabbage, carrots, cauliflower, collard greens, corn, green beans, parsley, potatoes, pumpkin, shiitake mushrooms, Swiss chard, turnips, wild mushrooms, winter squash, yams; adzuki beans, lentils, peas; almonds, peanuts; rye, oats, rice; apricots, figs, grapes, nectarines, plums, prunes, raspberries; olive oil, sesame oil; cheese, eggs.

Warming: chilies, leeks, onions, mustard greens, shallots, spring onions; black beans; pumpkin seeds, sesame seeds, sunflower seeds, walnuts; glutinous rice; cherries, dates, peaches; black pepper, cardamom, cinnamon, cloves, cumin, fennel seeds, fenugreek, garlic, ginger, mustard seed, nutmeg, oregano, tangerine peel, thyme, turmeric; sugar, wine; beef, chicken, lamb, marrow bones, salmon; butter.

COOKING METHODS

Cooling: no cooking (raw foods), blanching, steaming
Neutral: boiling
Warming: sautéing, stir-frying, baking, roasting, grilling, barbecuing

Western Ways to Keep the Body in Balance

Among other things, Western nutrition looks at the acid-alkaline balance of our bodies and what we eat. To keep our vital energy strong, we want the blood to be more alkaline than acidic. When we have an excess of acids, the body maintains its balance by depositing them in the joints and tissues, possibly creating such ailments as arthritis, muscle stiffness, nausea, tension, stomachaches, fatigue, ulcers, chest pain, and headaches. The normal, neutral pH range is between 7.35 and 7.45. But you don't need to be too scientific about it. You need only observe how you feel over a period of days or weeks as you try different foods, knowing which ones create acidic conditions and which ones create alkaline conditions. When you do this, you will see how easy it is to become too acidic. That's why the message these days is to eat more and more vegetables.

Foods that are acidifying: Cheese and other dairy products, most common grains and cereals (wheat, rye, barley, oats, and corn—rice is neutral), most beans, most nuts, oils, peanut butter, sugar, soft drinks, alcoholic beverages, drugs, meat, chicken, fish, junk food, black tea, coffee.

Foods that are alkalinizing: Fruits, vegetables, seaweeds, green algae, herbal teas, green tea, bancha tea, spices, raw honey, millet, buckwheat, quinoa, soaked and sprouted grains, raw almonds, almond butter, seeds (flax, sesame, sunflower, pumpkin), tofu, fermented foods, soy sauce, miso, umeboshi plums, salt, lima beans, adzuki beans. Deep breathing is also alkalinizing.

RECOMMENDED READING

Hobbs, Christopher, *Foundations of Health: Healing with Herbs and Food,* Botanica Press, 1992.

Hobbs, Christopher, *Herbal Remedies for Dummies,* Wiley, 1998.

Pitchford, Paul, *Healing with Whole Foods,* North Atlantic Books, 1993.

Tierra, Lesley, *Healing with the Herbs of Life,* Crossing Press, 2003.

Tierra, Michael, *The Way of Chinese Herbs,* Pocket Books, 1998.

Asian Crispy Fried Shallots

Makes about 1 cup (250 g)

10 shallots, peeled and thinly sliced, or 2 medium red onions, peeled and quartered

about ½ cup (125 ml) vegetable oil

METHOD

- Press shallots between towels to take out excess moisture.
- Heat oil in a skillet over medium-high heat until hot.
- Fry shallots, stirring, until reddish brown.
- Remove with a slotted spoon and lay on a paper towel to cool. Once cooled, they will be crisp.
- Store in airtight container.

Basmati Rice

Makes 2 cups rice (500 g)

This delicious, aromatic, easily digested rice is grown in the foothills of the Himalayas. An Indian meal is not complete without basmati rice.

1 cup (200 g) white basmati rice

slightly less than 2 cups (500 ml) water

pinch sea salt

METHOD

- Place rice in a medium bowl and rinse 3–4 times under cold water, straining between rinses.
- Put rice in a medium saucepan, add water and salt, and bring to a boil.
- Reduce heat to low, cover, and cook 15–20 minutes or until all water has been absorbed.
- Fluff rice with a fork before serving.

APPENDIX

Preparing the Basics

Homemade Seitan

Makes 6–8 pieces

2 cups (300 g) 80-percent wheat-gluten flour

1 teaspoon garlic powder

1 teaspoon ground ginger

½ teaspoon cumin

½ teaspoon turmeric

1¼ cups (310 ml) water or vegetable broth

3 tablespoons tamari or Bragg Liquid Aminos

1–3 teaspoons toasted sesame oil (optional)

BROTH

4 cups (1 L) water

¼ cup (60 ml) tamari

1 3-inch (7.5-cm) piece kombu seaweed

3 slices fresh ginger root

METHOD

- In a medium bowl, mix flour with garlic, ginger, cumin, and turmeric.
- Mix 1¼ cups (310 ml) water, 3 tablespoons tamari, and sesame oil together in another bowl and add to flour mixture
- Mix vigorously with a fork until a stiff dough forms.

- Knead dough 10–15 times and then let it rest 2–5 minutes. Knead a few more times and let it rest 15 minutes more.
- Cut gluten dough into 6–8 pieces, stretched into cutlets.
- Make broth: In a large pot, stir together 4 cups (1 L) water, ¼ cup (60 ml) tamari, kombu, and fresh ginger and bring to a boil.
- Reduce heat to low, drop in gluten pieces, cover, and cook 1 hour.
- Drain broth and reserve for soup. Cover seitan and store in the refrigerator for up to 1 week, or freeze for longer storage.

Crème Fraîche
(Soured Heavy Cream)
Makes 2 cups (500 ml)

Crème fraîche will not curdle in cooking. It is often used in French and Russian cuisine. You may substitute sour cream, Greek-style yogurt, or heavy cream, but be aware that they will curdle if the heat is too high.

2 cups (500 ml) heavy cream

3 tablespoons buttermilk or sour cream

METHOD

- Combine ingredients and whisk until well blended.
- Place in a jar, cover, and set aside at room temperature until cream sours and becomes very thick. This can take 8–24 hours, depending on temperature.
- Refrigerate. It will keep 10 days–2 weeks.

Homemade Yogurt

Makes 10 cups (2½ L)

A good source of amino acids and calcium, high-quality yogurt contains live active cultures that improve digestion. The cultures that turn milk into yogurt are *lactobacillus bulgaricus* and *streptococcus thermophilus*. People with milk allergies can sometimes tolerate yogurt because the fermentation process breaks down the milk protein. A staple in Indian and Middle Eastern cuisine, it can be used instead of butter to flavor and thicken sauces. To prevent curdling, mix it with a little flour before adding it. Yogurt may also be used as a substitute for milk, cream, buttermilk, mayonnaise, and sour cream in recipes.

1 gallon (4 L) milk, any kind
1 cup (250 g) plain yogurt with active
    cultures

METHOD

· Heat milk in a large pot over low heat.
· When milk is just warm (105° F or 40° C), remove from heat.
· Put already-prepared yogurt into a 1-quart (1-L) container.
· Add 1 cup (250 g) of warmed milk and stir.
· Pour this mixture into a 1-gallon (4-L) glass jar.
· Add remaining warmed milk, stir well with a wooden spoon, cap, and set to rest in a warm place 8–24 hours. The longer the yogurt sits, the easier it will be to digest.
· Refrigerate. It will keep 4–6 weeks.

Vegetable Stock

Makes 2 quarts (2 L)

1 onion, peeled and coarsely chopped
3 medium carrots, coarsely chopped
3 celery ribs with leaves, coarsely
    chopped
1 potato, coarsely chopped
8 ounces (250 g) white mushrooms
    or shiitake, coarsely chopped
6 black peppercorns
2 whole cloves
1 bay leaf
1 sprig fresh thyme
10 cups (2½ L) water
sea salt and freshly ground pepper

METHOD

· Bring water to a boil in a large pot over high heat.
· Stir in all ingredients, reduce heat to low, cover, and cook 2 hours.
· Strain stock through a colander and season to taste with salt and pepper.
· Store in the refrigerator or freeze.

Whole-Wheat Pie Crust

Makes bottom and top crust for a 9-inch (22.5-cm) pie

This dairy-free crust is very easy to prepare. All-purpose flour may be used instead of whole-wheat pastry flour.

1 cup (150 g) whole-wheat pastry flour
1 cup (150 g) unbleached pastry flour
⅓ cup (75 ml) vegetable oil
⅔ cup (150 ml) hot water

METHOD

· Put flour in a bowl.
· Mix oil and hot water together in a measuring cup.
· Pour liquid into flour and work quickly with hands to form a large ball.
· Divide dough in half. Flatten each part to a round, dust with flour, and roll out. If making a tart, simply push one part dough into pan with fingers (no need to roll out).

GLOSSARY
of Ingredients

Black sesame seeds: The Chinese use these seeds to treat the liver and kidneys, to lubricate the intestines, and to improve eyesight. They are good for overheated blood systems. They can be found in Chinese markets.

Bragg Liquid Aminos: This product is a pure, unfermented salt substitute made from water and soybeans. It contains all eight essential amino acids. It can be found in natural food stores.

Brewer's yeast: Also called nutritional yeast, brewer's yeast has been an important standby for vegetarians for many years. In addition to its abundant vitamin B12, lacking in vegetarian diets, it has a nutty flavor that complements brown rice and popcorn and tastes good in sauces. It can be used as a coating instead of flour for frying tofu.

Chilies, fresh: Chili peppers are very rich sources of iron and vitamins A and C. Most of the green chilies called for in this book are serranos, which are 2-4 inches (5-10 cm) long and about 1/3 inch (1.2 cm) thick. Jalapeños are different but may be used as a cooler substitute,

with their seeds removed. Look for chilies with smooth, tight skins and thick, meaty bodies. Store them in a cool place. Refrain from touching your eyes while handling chilies and wash your hands afterward—their capsaicin content is what gives chilies their bite and can sting sensitive tissue.

Dried tangerine peel: Used in Chinese cooking, dried tangerine peel has a warming energy that helps with digestion. Add a small piece to boiling rice, congee, teas, and stews.

Egg substitute: Use 1/4 cup (60 g) silken tofu per egg. Replace eggs in baked goods by adding 2 teaspoons baking powder per egg.

Fat: Margarine or other hydrogenated or partially hydrogenated oils are hard to digest and just plain bad for you. As much as possible, use high-quality oils and fats, such as cold-pressed extra virgin olive oil, canola oil, safflower oil, ghee (clarified butter), or organic butter. When a recipe calls for a lot of oil, replace it with a vegetable stock in cooked dishes and with yogurt in salads. For desserts, apple butter works well as a fat substitute.

Fermented foods: Fermented foods are commonly used all over the world. Though it may not sound very appetizing, the bacteria, fungus, or other organism growing in fermented foods actually improves their flavor, digestibility, and nutritional value, as well as acting as a preservative. After a course of antibiotics it's a good idea to eat fermented foods to replenish your beneficial intestinal

flora. Fermented foods include soy sauce, miso, tempeh, kimchi, beer, wine, hard and soft cheese, cottage cheese, yogurt, kefir, fromage blanc, crème fraîche, sauerkraut, pickles, and olives.

Flaxseed or linseed: Used in Germany as an ingredient in muesli, these reddish-brown seeds have mucilaginous property that helps lubricate and soothe the intestines and reduce flatulence. They also contain abundant vitamin E and essential fatty acids.

Garam masala: This common Indian seasoning can be found in Asian markets or made by grinding 1 tablespoon cardamom seeds, 1 stick cinnamon, 1 teaspoon cumin seeds, 1 teaspoon whole cloves, 1 teaspoon black peppercorns, and 1/2 teaspoon nutmeg (makes 3 tablespoons). It loses its flavor quickly, so make small quantities.

Garlic: Garlic has a warming energy that aids digestion and cleans the blood. It is also a good antibiotic and anti-inflammatory. Eat garlic in autumn, winter, and spring to prevent colds and flu and to help treat respiratory ailments. To use it, crush peeled cloves with a heavy knife. Press down on cloves using a back and forth motion. This action releases the essential oils. Then finely chop.

Ghee: Used daily throughout India and Southeast Asia, ghee is clarified butter, without any solid milk particles or water. A good-quality ghee imparts a pleasing flavor to food. According to ayurvedic medicine, ghee is the best cooking oil, in moderate amounts. Found in natural and ethnic food stores, it lasts a long time and does not need to be refrigerated. To make ghee, heat 1 pound (500 g) unsalted butter in a saucepan over medium-high heat until it starts to bubble; reduce heat to medium-low, cover, and cook until butter turns a clear golden yellow; skim off bubbly layer and store in a dry container at room temperature (*makes 2 cups or 500 g*).

Ginger root: Fresh ginger is the thick, vigorous, irregularly shaped root of a tropical plant. Used as a digestive aid, for motion sickness, and for sweating out colds and flus, ginger has a spicy flavor and is used frequently in Asian cuisine to warm the cooling energy of foods like tofu and vegetables. It should generally be very finely minced or grated. If used as a big chunk in cooking, it should be removed before serving the dish. A slice should be about 1 inch (2.5 cm) in diameter and ⅛ inch (3 mm) in thickness. To extract the juice, squeeze a slice or two in a garlic press. To crush, use the blade of a knife to press down. Store unused ginger root in a cool, dry place.

Miso: This fermented bean paste can be used to create a flavor similar to meat broth. Made from beans, grain, salt, and *Aspergillus orzyae* bacteria, it comes in a full range of flavors and colors. Unpasteurized miso contains 12–13 percent protein and lots of natural enzymes, which stimulate digestion. A sweet white miso and a brown miso are nice to have on hand in the pantry. Use about 1 tablespoon miso to 4 cups

(1 L) liquid. Do not boil miso; too much heat kills the bacteria.

Mung beans: These small green-skinned beans can be found in Asian markets. Cooking time is 1½ hours, or 30 minutes pressure-cooked. Mung beans also make good sprouted beans to add to stir-fries, salads, and soups.

Quark: Similar to yogurt but thicker, this fresh cheese is produced in Germany, Holland, and Great Britain. In recipes it may be replaced with Greek-style yogurt or fromage blanc.

Seeds, roasted: Roasting sesame, sunflower, and pumpkin seeds brings out their flavor. Spread them thinly in a dry skillet over medium heat, shaking the pan until seeds are slightly brown.

Sea vegetables: Think of seaweed as a kind of vegetable rather than an exotic new food. There are two families of seaweeds, brown and red. Both are very high in calcium, iron, B vitamins (including B12), vitamin A, potassium, magnesium, phosphorous, and iodine. They are also very alkaline, which helps to balance out an acidic system. Because of their high mineral content, they have a calming effect on the emotions. They have a cooling nature, and too much can create an overly cool body system, so it is best to eat them in moderation (twice a week is good) and to use them with warming foods such as ginger or onion. Chop a variety of them fine and mix with an herbal blend (for example, herbes de Provence); keep some in a jar by the

stove to add here and there to your cooking; mix some with your sea salt; or mix some with your mustard.

Tahini: Made by grinding sesame seeds, tahini can be found in natural food stores in raw or toasted form. The raw kind has a lighter flavor and is more versatile. It can be used instead of dairy to add creaminess and high-quality protein to dressings, sauces, dips, and soups. It complements grains very well, making a complete meal. Tahini needs to be thinned out with hot water before use.

Tofu: Bland-flavored but very versatile and rich in protein, tofu is made from curdled soy milk and is a common ingredient in Chinese and Japanese cuisines. Also known as bean curd, it comes in a variety of textures. Silken tofu is used for soups, dressings, dips, and beverages, while the firmer varieties are used for stir-fries, salads, broiling, and baking.

Turmeric: From the ginger family, this yellow powder is used for its color and its medicinal properties (anti-inflammatory) in Asian cuisine.

INDEX

of Ingredients

TABLE
of Equivalents

The following tables are approximate; they do not completely conform to official conversions.

A FEW RULES OF MEASURING

· Always stick religiously to one system; never mix and match.

· When measuring liquids, place the jug on a flat surface, bend down, and check for accuracy at eye level.

· When using a cup, spoon the ingredient into the cup, mounding slightly, and level off with the back of a knife. Do not use the cup as a scoop or tap the cup on the work surface.

Liquid Conversions

METRIC	IMPERIAL	US
30 ml	1 fl oz	2 tbsp
45 ml	1½ fl oz	3 tbsp
60 ml	2 fl oz	¼ cup
75 ml	2½ fl oz	⅓ cup
90 ml	3 fl oz	⅓ cup + 1 tbsp
100 ml	3½ fl oz	⅓ cup + 2 tbsp
125 ml	4 fl oz	½ cup
150 ml	5 fl oz	⅔ cup
175 ml	6 fl oz	¾ cup
200 ml	7 fl oz	¾ cup + 2 tbsp
250 ml	8 fl oz	1 cup
275 ml	9 fl oz	1 cup + 2 tbsp
300 ml	10 fl oz	1¼ cups
325 ml	11 fl oz	1⅓ cups
350 ml	12 fl oz	1½ cups
375 ml	13 fl oz	1⅔ cups
400 ml	14 fl oz	1¾ cups
450 ml	15 fl oz	1¾ cups + 2 tbsp
500 ml	16 fl oz	1 pint (2 cups)
600 ml	1 pint	2½ cups
900 ml	1½ pints	3¾ cups
1 liter	1¾ pints	4 cups

Weight Conversions

METRIC	UK/US
15 g	½ oz
30 g	1 oz
45 g	1½ oz
60 g	2 oz
75 g	2½ oz
90 g	3 oz
100 g	3½ oz
125 g	4 oz
150 g	5 oz
175 g	6 oz
200 g	7 oz
250 g	8 oz
275 g	9 oz
300 g	10 oz
325 g	11 oz
350 g	12 oz
375 g	13 oz
400 g	14 oz
450 g	15 oz
500 g	1 lb

Oven Temperatures

CELSIUS	FAHRENHEIT
120	250
140	275
150	300
160	325
180	350
190	375
200	400
220	425
230	450
240	475
260	500

Note: Reduce the temperature by 68° F (20° C) for fan-assisted ovens.

Useful Equivalents

3 tsp = 1 tbsp

2 tbsp = 1 oz

8 oz = 1 cup

2 cups = 1 pint

2 pints = 1 quart

4 quarts = 1 gallon

FLOUR OR DRIED BREAD CRUMBS

¼ cup = 1¼ oz

1 cup = 5 oz

3½ cups = 1 lb

WHITE SUGAR

1 cup = 8 oz

BROWN SUGAR

1 cup = 5½ oz

HONEY OR SYRUP

1 cup = 11 oz

GRATED CHEESE

1 cup = 4 oz

RICE

1 cup = 5 oz

DRIED BEANS

1 cup = 6 oz

Acknowledgments

I would first like to give all my gratefulness to the blessings of my Buddhist teacher Dzongsar Khyentse Rinpoche. It is through his blessings that this book ever got written. Without him, I would still be lost, running with my many ideas. It is through his teachings that my mind has begun to change. I also give my appreciation for my time in the kitchen at La Sonnerie in Dordogne, France, cooking for the great masters, and for the compassion and generosity of Pema Wangyal Rinpoche and Jigme Khyentse Rinpoche and the complete love and support that their family gives endlessly.

A special thank-you to my publishers, Maria Levy and Eric Swanson of Provecho Press. Everyone warned me that this would be hardest part, but working with these people was the easiest and most enjoyable. They knew intuitively what I wanted and carried it out effortlessly. Maria was a complete jewel to work with. She is an artist and always said yes to my wishes. Eric has the ability to get many things done and still act relaxed. He captured in his photos the artistic beauty I wished for the book. I thank their editing team, Peg Goldstein and Sarah Baldwin, for their keen eyes and ability to leave my voice in place. I thank them many times.

This book would not be a book without each person who shared his or her kitchen, recipe, and story with me. It was so much fun to be with each and every one of these wonderful people. I would like to thank them all: Fatima Ribiero, Aysa Whitney, Lucinda Denis, Daniel Denis, Mimi Snowden, Michael Tierra, Jeanne Anarelys, Elizabeth Edmunds, Mary Edmunds, Nadia Trochkova, Chokyi-la, Lucio Montido, Kemal Zengin, Marianne Denis, Erna Pelleprat, Atsuko Watanabe, Katie Malley, Carlos Middione, Tammy Semtchine, Janine Scotto, Diane Mooney, Josephine Araldo, Fran Dwyer, Yvonne Gold, Pamela Croci, Beharuz Attar, Gualter Guerriero, Zelia Guerriero, Begonia Llanos, Armel Ressot, Barbara Ma, Ting Adolphus, Janejira Binsri, Chanok Matenand, Cornellia Aihara, Maya Meyer, Eleanna Ianneloy, Hafida Bousouka, Fiona Nagel, Helen Jackson Jones, Fabienne Imbasciata, Anne and Marc Zansom, Claudia Salqueriruho, Lisa Davidson, Charlie Goodwin, Tsering Chhodern, Alysia Ann Lee, Ruchi Sharan, Florence So, Peggy Crayton, Patrick Jacquelin, Bridget Paumard, Francoise Iroas, Jeanette Colbot, Jean-Peirre Paumard, Loekito Hidajat, Steve Rempe, Megan Mooney, Beth Baugh, Diana Kennedy, Janine Karpeles, Leslie Fennern, Mary Garland, Georgianna Garland, Susan Garland, Elsie Forno, Lucie Abgrall, Doris Wolter, Tineke Adolphus, Cathy Hains, Rosana Arriaga, Herman Aihara, Cecile Emprou, Xou Le Roux, Jill Heald, Robin Eastick, Lama Tsering Everest, Serge Bruna-Rosso Atonne Pinschoff, Anne Tardy, Albert Paravi, Karla Olson, Marilyn Sollenberger, Yinwah Ma, and Wulstan Fletcher.

Since I have been cooking for some years, I have had the opportunity to learn from many wonderful chefs. Josephine Araldo was the best gift that came my way. She really opened my way to cooking and the joy of a culinary herb garden. For my herb and health education, I would like to give my appreciation to Christopher Hobbs, Beth Baugh (for her cooking, too), and Michael and Leslie Tierra. A thank-you to my children, Patrick and Katie Malley, for eating their mom's cooking over the years and for making me need to cook every day, thus helping me learn to know what they appreciated and what they hated. To my mother and father, who always fed me well and gave me the opportunities to be exposed to the taste of good food. To my friends—Sandra Scales, Yvonne Gold, Juliet Prentice, and Margaret Loyan—who were there when I needed the push, support, and clarity.

I appreciate all the help I have been given and would like to quote from Nagarjuna, a great Indian master who expounded the teachings of the Middle Way: "May Bodhicitta,* precious and sublime, arise where it has not yet come to be, and where it has arisen may it never fail, but grow and flourish ever more and more."

*Bodhicitta: the aspiration to benefit others with love, compassion, and wisdom, and the putting of that aspiration into action.

༄༅། སྟོན་པ་བླ་མེད་སངས་རྒྱས་རིན་པོ་ཆེ། །སྐྱོབ་པ་བླ་མེད་དམ་ཆོས་རིན་པོ་ཆེ། །འདྲེན་པ་བླ་མེད་དགེ་འདུན་རིན་པོ་ཆེ། །སྐྱབས་གནས་དཀོན་མཆོག་གསུམ་ལ་མཆོད་པ་འབུལ།། །།

༄༅། །སྟོན་པ་བླ་མེད་སངས་རྒྱས་རིན་པོ་ཆེ། །
སྐྱོབ་པ་བླ་མེད་དམ་ཆོས་རིན་པོ་ཆེ། །
འདྲེན་པ་བླ་མེད་དགེ་འདུན་རིན་པོ་ཆེ། །
སྐྱབས་གནས་དཀོན་མཆོག་གསུམ་ལ་མཆོད་པ་འབུལ།། །།

❀

Tönpa lamé sangyé rinpoché
To the precious Buddha, teacher unsurpassed

Kyob-pa lamé tamchö rinpoché
To the precious Dharma, unsurpassed protection

Drenpa lamé gendun rinpoché
To the precious Sangha, unsurpassed guides

Kyabné könchok sum la chöpar bul.
To the triple place of refuge, I offer this nourishment.